DILIGENT AND UNWEARIED IN THE
DISCHARGE OF HIS PASTORAL DUTIES:

The 1805 Diary
of the
Rev. Dr. James Muir
MINISTER OF THE OLD PRESBYTERIAN
MEETING HOUSE IN ALEXANDRIA, VIRGINIA

Editing, Annotations, and
Supplementary Information
by
Donald C. Dahmann

HERITAGE BOOKS
2011

HERITAGE BOOKS
AN IMPRINT OF HERITAGE BOOKS, INC.

Books, CDs, and more—Worldwide

For our listing of thousands of titles see our website
at
www.HeritageBooks.com

Published 2011 by
HERITAGE BOOKS, INC.
Publishing Division
100 Railroad Ave. #104
Westminster, Maryland 21157

Copyright © 2011 Donald C. Dahmann

Cover: Portrait of the Rev. Dr. James Muir
(Pastel by William Joseph Williams, 1798)

All rights reserved. No part of this book may be reproduced or transmitted in any form or by any means, electronic or mechanical, including photocopying, recording or by any information storage and retrieval system without written permission from the author, except for the inclusion of brief quotations in a review.

International Standard Book Numbers
Paperbound: 978-0-7884-5304-5
Clothbound: 978-0-7884-8710-1

"The first idea was not our own. Adam
In Eden was the father of Descartes
And Eve made air the mirror of herself,

Of her sons and of her daughters. They found themselves
In Heaven as in a glass; a second Earth;
And in the earth itself they found a green —

The inhabitants of a very varnished green.
But the first idea was not to shape the clouds
In imitation. The clouds preceded us.

There was a muddy centre before we breathed.
There was a myth before the myth began,
Venerable and articulate and complete.

From this the poem springs: that we live in a place
That is not our own and, much more, not ourselves
And hard it is in spite of blazoned days.

We are the mimics. Clouds are pedagogues… "

   Wallace Stevens, from *Notes Toward a Supreme Fiction* (1942)

"Therefore, since we are surrounded by so great a cloud of witnesses, let us also lay aside every weight and the sin that clings so closely, and let us run with perseverance the race that is set before us… "

   Letter to the Hebrews 12:1, *The Bible* (NRSV)

Contents

Preface and Acknowledgements	viii

Part I. INTRODUCTION

1.	Alexandria in 1805 and Rev. Dr. Muir's Diary	1
2.	The Rev. Dr. James Muir	10
3.	The Original Diary and Its Transcription	17

Part II. THE REV. DR. JAMES MUIR'S DIARY	21

Part III. APPENDICES

A.	Title Page and Handwritten Notes Appearing on End Pages of Diary	89
B.	Bible Texts of Sermons by Rev. Dr. Muir during 1805, in the Order Delivered	94
C.	Published Works of Rev. Dr. James Muir	95
D.	Alexandria's Old Presbyterian Meeting House	102
	Bibliography	106
	Index	117

List of Illustrations

1. Portrait of the Rev. Dr. James Muir. (Pastel by William Joseph Williams courtesy of the Old Presbyterian Meeting House)   11

2. Page of Rev. Dr. Muir's 1805 Diary with Entries for 16 to 19 June. (Courtesy of the Old Presbyterian Meeting House)   19

3. The Old Presbyterian Meeting House at Alexandria, Virginia Today. (Drawing by Betty Heiby courtesy of the artist and Old Presbyterian Meeting House)   105

Preface and Acknowledgements

Two centuries after it was written, the 1805 diary of the Rev. Dr. James Muir now opens a window into the life of a Presbyterian minister eight generations ago. Born in Ayrshire, Scotland in 1757, Rev. Muir served as the third minister of the Presbyterian Church in Alexandria, Virginia, now known as the Old Presbyterian Meeting House, from 1789 until his death in 1820. Remembered as a significant figure in the history of Alexandria, his career otherwise, except for one or two of his publications, has largely receded into the shadows (Stauffer 1918, Reinhold 1968, Smylie 1972-73, Dickson 1987). The year 1805 has dropped into similar obscurity. Nonetheless, it stands out in American history in several respects – the first and only justice of the U.S. Supreme Court, Samuel Chase, was impeached and acquitted, setting numerous precedents – Muir follows the trial in his diary during February and March; the United States successfully asserted its naval and military power overseas in the engagements known as the First Barbary War, which was concluded in June (Lambert 2005, Toll 2006); and the most important geographic expedition ever sponsored by the federal government, the Corps of Discovery headed by Captains Meriwether Lewis and William Clark, succeeded in crossing the continent – it reached the Pacific Ocean in November (Moulton 1983-2001, Ambrose 1996).

This volume provides an annotated transcription of the personal diary Rev. Muir kept during 1805; an introduction to the period and place in which it was written; an overview of Rev. Muir's life and bibliography of his published works; a list of the Bible texts on which Rev. Muir based the sermons he delivered in 1805; and a brief history of the congregation he served.

The assistance of Thomas E. Camden, director of Special Collections, Library of Virginia, enabled the first steps in the creation of this project to be taken, and is much appreciated – he literally opened the door to our learning of the existence of the almanac-diary. Thanks are also due the Library of Virginia as an institution for its preservation of the original almanac-diary and for its continuing commitment to preserving the heritage of the Commonwealth of Virginia.

The first draft of the transcription emerged from a group effort that included Barbara R. Evans, Deborah Farmer, Dacia Stalker, and Donald C. Dahmann. The initial transcription was then edited and annotated by Donald C. Dahmann, who also provided the supplementary materials. The volume was brought into its final form in the Archive of the Old Presbyterian Meeting House, which, from 1787 to 1899, served as the parlor of the Meeting House parsonage – the residence of the Muir family from 1789 to 1823. No doubt Rev. Muir made diary entries while seated in this very room!

The transcription's final form incorporates many useful comments and suggestions received from George Combs and others of the Local History-Special Collections Branch, Alexandria Library; Frederick H. Morhart, Susan Morhart, Eleanor K. Pourron, David C. McGarvey, and Hugh M. Van Horn, members of the Old Presbyterian Meeting House; and Professor Dewey D. Wallace, George Washington University. The support and encouragement provided by the History and Archives Committee of the Old Presbyterian Meeting House throughout the preparation of this volume helped made it a cheerful task. The final version benefited immensely from close readings by Deborah Farmer and Hugh Van Horn, both members of the Meeting House History and Archives Committee.

The silhouette of the Rev. Dr. Muir that appears on the cover and the title page is reproduced from his book, *Ten Sermons*, published by Peter Cottom and James A. Stewart in Alexandria in 1812. The portrait of Rev. Muir that appears on the cover and as Figure 1 is a pastel drawn from life by William Joseph Williams in 1798 that was prepared for the Muir family. Williams (1759-1823), artist, miniaturist, and tradesman, worked in Eastern Seaboard cities from New York to Charleston, South Carolina. The portrait was donated to the Old Presbyterian Meeting House by James Stewart Huston of Coatesville, Pennsylvania, a relative of Rev. Muir's, and is used here with the permission of the Old Presbyterian Meeting House. The image of the Meeting House that appears on the cover and as Figure 3 is the work of Betty Heiby, a member of the Old Presbyterian Meeting House congregation. It was drawn in 1974 and is used with her permission.

Part I. INTRODUCTION

1. Alexandria in 1805 and Rev. Dr. Muir's Diary

On the twelfth of April 1805, Rev. Dr. James Muir turned 48 years of age. He had served Alexandria's congregation of Presbyterians for sixteen years – half of the thirty-one years he would eventually serve here. The diary he maintained that year depicts the life of a Presbyterian minister during the early nineteenth-century by a man who was remembered by his colleagues as possessing "an exceedingly well balanced, well disciplined, and well furnished mind... [with] an air of loveliness and simplicity about him [whose] sermons were always full of vigorous and condensed thought" (Sprague *et al.* 1858). He was remembered by his congregation as "amiable and unobtrusive in his manners, kind and benevolent in his disposition, diligent and unswerving in the discharge of his pastoral duties" (Muir memorial in the Old Presbyterian Meeting House). The final clause of the congregation's tribute serves as the title of this transcription of the diary he maintained in 1805.

Rev. Muir's diary provides a historical document that, in its account of a single calendar year in the life of one individual, both raises and answers questions about a bygone era. It raises questions for our contemporary period as well. And it provides a historical guide to aspects of the remarkable heritage that continues in Old Town Alexandria, Virginia, a heritage that exists today in the vibrant religious community of the Old Presbyterian Meeting House and the larger community, where numerous elements of Rev. Muir's story, including homes, businesses, streetscapes, and institutions continue not only to exist, but to function and flourish.

While serving as the minister of the Presbyterian congregation in Alexandria, Rev. Muir, his wife, Elizabeth Welman Muir, their four children, and a servant lived in the parsonage provided by the congregation, located in the 300-block of South Royal Street. The Meeting House where the Presbyterians worshipped is in the 300-block of South Fairfax Street, on the opposite end of today's churchyard from the parsonage (McGroarty 1940a, Internet site– www.opmh.org). The parsonage was erected in 1787 by Robert Brockett, a local builder and member of the Meeting House congregation. It is now known as Flounder House. When the Muirs resided there, the yard of the parsonage was separated from the churchyard by a fence. The parsonage of Rev. Muir's time included three and one-half floors of living space – a full basement plus two and one-half floors above ground. Rev. Muir described it as a "commodious house," an assessment that many would find surprising today (Larkin 2006).

The Muir's son, Samuel Crichton Muir, then sixteen years of age, spent most of 1805 away from home while studying at a school conducted by the Rev. William Maffitt, a Presbyterian minister. The school was conducted at the Maffitt estate, Chantilly, 35 miles west of Alexandria in Fairfax County. Prior to studying with Rev. Maffitt at Chantilly, Samuel had attended the Alexandria Academy, which Rev. Maffitt had headed before moving to Chantilly. The three Muir daughters – Jane Wardlaw Muir, seventeen, Mary Wardlaw Muir, eleven, and Elizabeth Love Muir, five – were all at home during 1805. The two older daughters attended the Alexandria Academy during the school year, and all three no doubt were home schooled by their mother, a well-educated woman, as well (Allen 1996-97, 2001). During the year, Mary also traveled to Bermuda to visit her maternal grandparents and other members of the Welman family.

Entries in Rev. Muir's diary and in congregational records indicate that 1805 was a typical year in his Alexandria ministry. It was filled with events that one would expect to occur in the life of a Presbyterian minister serving a congregation located in a relatively large, growing, and economically prosperous eastern seaport upon entering the nineteenth century. As is always normal for clergy, much of his time was occupied with providing pastoral care to members of the congregation and in the preparation of sermons. He was also actively engaged in visiting others in need and in assisting in the affairs of the Alexandria Academy and the Alexandria Library Company.

Rev. Muir's congregation embodied a cross-section of the residents of the town – it included families from the full spectrum of incomes and urban occupations, from among the wealthiest members of the community to those who were poor; it included landed gentry and merchant princes owning both a town house and country estate, and blacksmiths and dock workers who resided on the waterfront; it included men who had served as soldiers, officers, quartermasters, and doctors in the French and Indian War and the Revolutionary War; it included those who had lived in Alexandria for fifty years and those who had just arrived, most typically from Scotland, England, the Middle Atlantic or New England states; it included abolitionists and slave-owners, and African Americans, both enslaved and freedmen. It was a diverse urban congregation.

Alexandria had been established in 1749 as the Colony of Virginia's farthest inland port town on the Potomac River. Not far downriver from the Great Falls of the Potomac, the town sat on a bluff above a deep-water port. It served as the primary transportation and commercial center exporting agricultural products from the western portion of Virginia's Northern Neck and the rich Shenandoah Valley to markets in Europe and the West Indies, and importing goods from other ports on the Eastern Seaboard and overseas. In 1805, Alexandria was part of the newly created federal enclave of the District of Columbia – it had become part of the 100-square-mile federal district when that independent jurisdiction was created in 1800, and would remain part of it until that portion of the District located south of the Potomac River was returned to the Commonwealth of Virginia in 1847.

The port of Alexandria prospered. The first federal census of population, conducted in 1790, reported that it had 2,750 residents. This did not place it among the new nation's first tier of urban places – Philadelphia, New York City, Boston, Charleston, and Baltimore each possessed over 10,000 residents. Alexandria was only twenty-second in size, but it possessed great economic promise if the Potowmack Canal, and the later the Chesapeake and Ohio Canal, could connect the waters of the Atlantic with the Ohio River, where the new nation's emerging settlement frontier lay (Achenbach 2004).

Between 1790 and 1800, Alexandria's population grew 80 percent to 5,000 residents, and by 1810 an additional 45 percent to over 7,000. In the 1820s, however, New York's Erie Canal was completed, enabling New York City to gain the continentally dominant position it would never lose. But in 1805, when English businessman Robert Sutcliff referred to this place as "a beautiful little city," it was still very much in competition with its northern economic rivals (Sutcliff 1811). This seaport town connected the agriculturally rich areas of Northern Virginia and Shenandoah Valley with ports in Europe, Britain, and the West Indies, and was led by enterprising merchants fully expecting only the best for its future (Peterson 1932, Hurst 1991, Shomette 2003, Smith and Miller 1989).

Like other port towns of the day, Alexandria was physically compact and focused on the waterfront, the most critical element of the economy and the hub of a wide range of activities associated with the transshipping of goods on and off ships, servicing vessels, and the manufacture of shipping-related products ranging from the baking of biscuits to the production of rope. It was a walking city. Walking was the dominant means of local transportation – you could easily walk to any locale within town and much that lay outside as well, street and road conditions permitting. In its overall dimensions, Alexandria extended no more than a mile along the Potomac and about a half-mile inland. The bell atop the Presbyterian Meeting House, the only public bell in town until 1817, served as a community-wide signaling device. With many of its structures built of brick, including the Meeting House, parsonage, and numerous private homes, and with its paved streets intersecting at right angles, numerous visitors remarked that it looked like a smaller version of Philadelphia (Janson 1807, Massie 1922, Caldwell 1951).

Alexandria also possessed a diverse residential population for its size, similar in some ways to the larger urban centers it emulated. While ports were almost always more diverse than market towns, Alexandria was also a regional border town – the border between agricultural economies based on free and slave labor – and it drew migrants from both regions. Diversity existed along many dimensions, including religious affiliation. Alexandria's initial religious denomination was, of course, the Church of England, as it was the officially established religion in the Colony of Virginia, even if all were not necessarily true adherents to this denomination. The first Alexandria-based parish centered on a chapel of ease, constructed during the 1750s, and then later on the Church of England (today's Christ Episcopal Church), which was completed in 1773 (McKim 1894, Morrison 1979). Local Presbyterians initially worshiped at the Church of England, as by law they were required to do. But being Scots in a largely "Scottish" town, these Presbyterians also conducted informal services in their homes, then formal worship services at the town's Assembly Hall from the 1760s, and finally established a formal congregation with permanent clergy in 1772 (McGroarty 1940a, Sengel 1973, www.opmh.org). Adherents to other denominations soon followed in establishing their own congregations: the local Methodist congregation dates from 1774 (Stukenbroeker 1974, Hedman 1974); the Roman Catholic congregation, the earliest in the Commonwealth of Virginia, from 1795 (Guy 1995); the Religious Society of Friends (Quakers) from 1802 (Bromberg and Shepard 2006, Anderberg and Motheral 1996); and the initial Baptist congregation from 1803 (Fletcher 2003, Wallace 2003).

Difficult as it may be for us to imagine today, the daily lives of some individuals in 1805 were just as full as many perceive their lives to be in the twenty-first century. Rev. Muir was certainly one of those who maintained a very full schedule. His days were spent preparing discourses (sermons) to be delivered at two or three different worship services every Sunday (his diary includes the Biblical texts on which these were based); leading mid-week prayer-worship services in the evening; preaching at other Presbyterian congregations when their pulpits might be vacant (particularly within the local presbytery, which extended from Northern Virginia to north of Baltimore) and at places as far away as Norfolk, Virginia in developing new congregations; conducting baptismal, marriage, and funeral services, all separate from regular worship services; conducting charity sermons to raise money in support of the needy in the larger community; visiting members of the congregation in their homes; preparing for and attending a host of meetings concerning both church-related and community-related affairs; personal study; and engaging in an extensive exchange of correspondence (Smith 1962, Thompson 1963).

In addition to these routine activities, he prepared commentaries for publication in two newly established religious journals during the year – an eleven-installment piece, "The Decalogue" (The Ten Commandments), which appeared in the initial year of issue of the New England religious journal, *Panoplist*; and a four-installment piece, "Nebuchadnezzar," for the newly established journal sponsored by the Presbyterian Church, *General Assembly's Missionary Magazine; or, Evangelical Intelligencer*. He used the pseudonym "Philologos" (Lover of the Word) in authoring these two series. In subsequent years, he would prepare two more articles for the *Panoplist*, and two more for the *Missionary Magazine* (see Appendix A for list of his publications).

In terms of literary style, Rev. Muir's diary can at best be described as straight forward. It is as though entries were made to record no more than the facts relating to events and actions in order simply to have written reminders at hand should they be needed at a later date. Entries provide little in the way of interpretation of the events being recorded. Explicit emotion appears rarely. In one instance (on the 7th of August), he records a single-word outburst in response to a death resulting from a duel that took place locally – "disgraceful" (underscored in the diary). In conjunction with preaching at a Sunday morning worship service on the 8th of August, he notes – "Feeling uncommon freedom" – perhaps the same sensation that the great evangelist George Whitefield described as "a freedom in preaching," which he experienced while addressing a crowd in New York City (Burrows and Wallace 1999).

The diary was certainly not prepared to entertain readers two-hundred years after it was written! Nonetheless, it does captivate, as entries touch on such a broad range of topics and, like any first-hand account, provide details of a true eyewitness. The diary is not just a historic document, but empirical first-hand evidence of the very substance of life that is required to interpret not only Rev. Muir's life and his circumstances, but that of his contemporaries as well. The diary notes interactions with more than one hundred different persons during the year, in a wide range of situations – at dinners, at meetings, via correspondence, and the like. Most of these individuals are identified in the notes that accompany diary entries.

While written for personal purposes, the diary reveals numerous aspects of Presbyterian congregational life at the beginning of the nineteenth century – midweek evening prayer-worship services; celebration of the Lord's Supper with a "fenced" Table ("fenced" meaning "guarded" to preclude participation by any who may have been found to be unworthy of such by the congregation's Session) and a preceding "Action Sermon" (a sermon to prepare congregants for the "action" of consuming the Lord's Supper); forenoon, afternoon, and candlelight (evening) worship services every Lord's Day (Melton 1967); "reasonable revivals," which would include multiple worship services over consecutive days designed to promote soul searching among congregants (Thomas 1983); and the circulation of religious periodicals and books within the congregation and larger community, including such tomes as Richard Watson's six-volume *A Collection of Theological Tracts* (Watson 1791), and Johann Lorenz Mosheim's six-volume *An Ecclesiastical History: Antient* (sic) *and Modern, From the Birth of Christ, to the Beginning of the Present Century* (Mosheim 1797-98). The local exchange network for books and periodicals in which he participated was continuously energized with new materials obtained from local booksellers and from items arriving via the postal service or hand delivery from elsewhere, including overseas.

Rev. Muir regularly baptized and performed memorial and funeral services for members of the congregation, but his diary's record of the marriage, baptism, and funeral services that he performed during the year is only selective. He separately maintained a minister's book in which he recorded such services. It is preserved in transcription as *Register of Baptisms, Marriages, and Funerals during the Ministry of the Revd. Doctr. James Muir in the Presbyterian Church of Alexandria, D.C.* It provides information on numerous other marriage, baptism, and funeral services that he performed during the year that were not recorded in his personal diary. Other clergy also performed these services for members of the Meeting House congregation while the Rev. Muir was out of town.

The ardors of travel are revealed. Two journeys within Northern Virginia suggest the difficulties of travel in 1805 – the time of travel for two trips by horseback from Alexandria to Chantilly, location of the estate of the Rev. William Maffitt and his wife, Henrietta Turberville Maffitt, are recorded. These journeys over a distance of about 35 miles took five hours in April, and six hours in December. Despite the challenges presented by the period's poor road conditions, Rev. Muir traveled multiple times during the year to Georgetown and Baltimore, as well as taking one extended trip to Philadelphia, Princeton, New York City, and Connecticut. Long-distance travel between cities most often consisted of overnight rides in stage coaches. Rev. Muir's social and professional connections were even more far flung than his travels. They included regular exchanges of correspondence extending not only throughout Northern Virginia, but also to South Carolina, New England, Bermuda, and Britain.

The diary also provides information on Rev. Muir's engagement with current events. He notes the results of Alexandria's town council election, recording the names of all who were elected, and some of the complications encountered in conducting the election. He notes in some detail a local "theatre trial," to use his terminology. The impeachment trial of Supreme Court Associate Justice Samuel Chase by the U.S. Senate, an early partisan political confrontation, is closely followed. The death of British Admiral Lord Nelson – simply "Ld. Nelson" in the diary – at the Battle of Trafalgar is recorded on the 20th of December. European affairs received extensive coverage in Alexandria's newspaper throughout the year.

At times, daily events and actions taken by the Presbyterian Church cover common ground – on January the sixth, Rev. Muir responds to the sentencing of the seconds from the duel between Alexander Hamilton and Aaron Burr that had occurred the previous year; he attends meetings of the Presbytery of Baltimore at which dueling is condemned on the third of April; and he comments on a local duel that takes the life of an Alexandrian on the seventh of August. A local newspaper article from 1805 provides a measure of the high level of concern that existed over dueling as a societal evil – "President Dwight on Duelling (sic)," a 1,500-word essay by the Rev. Timothy Dwight IV (1752-1817), president of Yale College (see diary entry for the 12th of June).

Alexandria's weather could be miserable, most especially perhaps in winter. The Potomac River freezes solid during the winter of 1804-05 – "shutting up" the river is the term used in the diary – and stops the flow of cargo that Alexandria's port depends upon. Winter winds from the northwest are also noted – cold and harsh in 1805, they can be so today as well. Wet weather, which produced abominable walking conditions in Alexandria's unpaved streets, caused the cancellation of worship services several times. The good news of summer weather in Alexandria, that no one freezes to death, is welcome, but the hot, humid, and hazy days of Mid-Atlantic summers that Rev. Muir experienced were miserable – they remain miserable today even with air conditioning. Recorded temperatures in July 1805 were in the mid- and upper-90s, misery that was then experienced without respite.

Rev. Muir's diary records no explicit reference to his wife, Elizabeth Welman Muir, but he does note a regular correspondence with members of her family in Bermuda, including the fact that he sends them shipments of Jamieson's crackers, one of Alexandria's most famous locally produced items. We learn something about their children: about the journey of Mary to Bermuda; of Samuel's schooling by the Rev. William Maffitt at Chantilly; and of the purchase of bonnets for the two older daughters. Most deliciously, American eels (*Anguilla rostrata*), which once accounted for twenty-five percent of all fish harvested from the Potomac River, but are now rare, make an appearance, in conjunction with son Samuel's "eeling." The Muir family even engages in an activity that we perhaps think of as not emerging until our own "modern" times – they obtain carry-out food from Gadsby's Tavern, a leg of mutton for a meal with unexpected house guests.

Rev. Muir's diary provides many entertaining perspectives on urban life in America two centuries ago; insights into the early nineteenth-century lives of Presbyterian clergy; perspectives on one of early Alexandria's most active prominent citizens; and perhaps even raises questions for us in the twenty-first century. Upon reading this diary, I suspect that you will wish that you could hear Rev. Muir preach, and then invite him to your own home for dinner, at least once.

2. The Rev. Dr. James Muir

James Muir was born to George and Isobell (Wardlaw) Muir on April 12, 1757 at the parsonage of the Presbyterian Church at Cumnock, in Ayrshire, Scotland (the image in Fig. 1 shows him at forty-two years of age). The Rev. Dr. George Muir (1723-1771) had been a lawyer prior to being called to the ministry. He served Church of Scotland congregations at Cumnock from 1752 to 1766 and the High Kirk at Paisley from 1766 until his death in 1771. The Rev. Dr. John Witherspoon, who served Paisley's Low Kirk from 1758 until departing to become President of the College of New Jersey (now Princeton University) in the United States in 1768, was known to the young James during his youth in Paisley. James Muir's mother, Isobell, was the daughter of the Rev. James Wardlaw (1673-1742), another minister in the Church of Scotland. The family of George and Isobell Muir included five children who survived to adulthood: Anna Muir, James Muir, George Muir, Ebenezer Muir, and Jean Muir. George and Isobell Muir died within a year of each other in 1771. James was fourteen years of age and just about to enter college.

James Muir's formal education included studies at the universities at Glasgow and Edinburgh. He received the Masters of Arts (M.A.) degree upon completion of a five-year course of classical and philosophical studies at the University of Glasgow in 1776. His formal theological training was taken at the University of Edinburgh. He completed preparation for the ministry with his cousin, the Rev. Dr. Henry Hunter, minister of the Scots Church on London Wall Road in the City of London, and was licensed as a probationer in 1779. He then served London's Scots Church as assistant to Rev. Hunter and taught school for two years prior to accepting a call from the Christ Church (Church of Scotland) congregation in Bermuda in 1781 (Smith *et al*. 1984). He served the Bermuda congregation for seven years, and once again taught school, at what is now the Warwick Academy, which had been founded in 1662.

While serving in Bermuda, Rev. Muir married Elizabeth Welman (1766-1831) of Warwick, on the twenty-ninth of February 1783. Their marriage of thirty-seven years was broken only

Figure 1. Portrait of the Rev. Dr. James Muir.
(Pastel by William Joseph Williams, 1798)

by his death in 1820. Elizabeth Welman Muir was also well-educated. Following the death of her husband, she would conduct the Boarding and Day School for Young Ladies, together with her three daughters, at the corner of Prince and Washington streets in Alexandria. Following her death in 1831, the daughters continued the school for several decades. The Muir family included seven children, four of whom survived to adulthood – Jane Wardlaw Muir (1788-1862), Samuel Crichton Muir (1789-1832), Mary Wardlaw Muir (1794-1862), and Elizabeth Love Muir (1800-1876).

Rev. Muir's family left Bermuda in 1788 and relocated to New York City, where James served for nearly a year under the Rev. Dr. John Rodgers (1727-1811) in a temporary position at both the Wall Street (later First) Presbyterian Church and the Brick Presbyterian Church. In March 1789, Rev. Muir received a call from the Presbyterian congregation in Alexandria to serve as its minister. He served as the third installed minister of the Meeting House for the remaining thirty-two years of his life. During his long and distinguished ministry, he maintained an active involvement both within the Presbyterian Church – the Meeting House congregation, Presbytery of Baltimore, Synod of Philadelphia, and General Assembly – and within the local community – Alexandria, the District of Columbia, of which Alexandria was a part from 1800 to 1847, and Northern Virginia.

He expanded the congregation's involvement in mission work and Christian education, both then only beginning to emerge in the United States, and was involved in founding the Bible Society of the District of Columbia in 1814, two years before the creation of the American Bible Society (Muir 1814, Wosh 1994); a Sabbath Day School at the Meeting House in 1816, one of the earliest in a southern state (Boylan 1988); and the Onesimus Society, to organize support for the destitute, in 1816.

Rev. Muir was also instrumental in founding and then directing several other local organizations – the Alexandria Society for the Promotion of Useful Knowledge, established in 1790; the Alexandria Library Company, forerunner of the current Alexandria Library, which was established in 1794 (Seale 2007); the Alexandria Relief Society (Relief Fire Co.), also established in 1794, which housed its engines in the Meeting House churchyard (McKenney 1958); the Washington Society of Alexandria, established in 1800 to honor George Washington and perpetuate his legacy of financial support for the Alexandria Academy (McGroarty 1928); and Alexandria's Board of Guardians of the Free Schools, established in 1811.

During all of his years in Alexandria, the Rev. Muir served on the board of trustees of the Alexandria Academy, which had been founded in 1785 as Alexandria's first effort at providing education for the general public. As the long-time president of the board of trustees and head of its committee of overseers, he regularly communicated with George Washington, the school's major benefactor (Eaves 1936, McGroarty 1940b 1940c and 1941, Morgan 1977, Morrill 1987). Muir also communicated with Washington regularly in response to Washington's annual contribution to Alexandria's Poor Relief Committee, which he headed (Muir n.d.).

When Alexandria was threatened with attack by a British naval squadron during the War of 1812, Rev. Muir traveled to Washington, along with Charles Simms, town mayor, and Dr. Elisha Cullen Dick, to negotiate the town's fate with General Robert Ross and Admiral George Cockburn. Washington had already been captured and burned by the British. Alexandria, which lay undefended, was surrendered to the British. Its warehouses bountifully served to reprovision the British fleet, but the town remained otherwise unharmed (Herrick 2005).

For thirty years, Rev. Muir also served as chaplain of Alexandria's St. Andrew's Society and of the Alexandria-Washington Masonic Lodge No. 22, which George Washington once served as grand master (Brockett and Uhler 1899). He delivered numerous charity sermons to raise money to assist those in need, on behalf of these and other organizations. He also participated in ceremonies setting the initial boundary marker of the District of Columbia at Jones Point, the southernmost extent of Alexandria, in 1791 (Muir 1791), and in laying the cornerstone of the U.S. Capitol in the District of Columbia in 1793.

Rev. Muir's numerous published works appeared as pamphlets, as analytic pieces and commentaries in journals, and as books. Many of his publications initially were delivered as sermons, or as discourses, as they were also appropriately termed. Presbyterian worship services in Alexandria on the Sabbath – the "Lord's Day" to use the term employed by Rev. Muir in his diary – consisted of a forenoon service (commencing at 11:00 a.m.), an afternoon service (beginning at 4:00 p.m.), and an evening service (beginning about 6:30 p.m.) also known as the service "at candle light."

Both of the two daytime services included a formal sermon (the diary notes Bible texts), and all three services, intended for the entire congregation, were more of a single Lord's Day service conducted in three parts, a stark contrast with the contemporary pattern of Sunday worship. Today, congregations are offered multiple services, but with very few exceptions, worshippers attend only the one found most convenient to their personal schedules. Each service in Rev. Muir's day was announced with a "call to worship" by the church bell striking one-quarter hour prior to the beginning of service. Sundays for Presbyterians in Alexandria, as was true throughout much of the Middle Atlantic states and New England, continued to mean observation of the "Puritan Sabbath" – a day to come before God in multiple public worship services; to privately spend time in quiet contemplation and study; to refrain from tasks involving hard physical labor; and absolutely not to participate in events such as horse racing, gaming, or other frivolities (Solberg 1977, Larkin 1988).

For Rev. Muir, preaching each Lord's Day at forenoon, afternoon, and evening worship services meant the presentation of a discourse, a scholarly argument based on a Biblical text. Judging from his surviving discourses, Rev. Muir did not avoid directly confronting societal concerns of the day. He stood squarely in the jeremiad tradition commonly associated with New England Puritanism, calling for confessions of waywardness and communal repentance to sustain the protection of God for both individuals and the nation (Nash 1965, Gribbin 1971, Smylie 1972-73, Dickson 1978, Bercovitch 1978, Laha 2002). The Rev. Dr. William R. Sengel, one of his twentieth-century successors in the Meeting House pulpit, noted as well that Muir "pointed as often to judgment as to mercy" (Sengel 1973 p. 43).

An excerpt from one of his discourses demonstrates the flavor of Rev. Muir's preaching. With former President George Washington among those assembled at the Meeting House to publicly observe a National Day of Solemn Humiliation, Fasting, and Prayer on the ninth of May 1798, he closed his remarks with these words:

> Whilst this day we bewail the degraded state into which many among us are sunk; whilst we bewail the neglect of religion whence that degradation originates; whilst we confess our sins, and deprecate the punishment which our sins deserve, let us not overlook those rays which gild the

threatened cloud. We have amongst us true patriots. Both the present and the late Presidents know the true interests of their country, and did, and still do steadily adhere to that interest. We have many who from the purest motives support our happy government; some who were misled have returned to just principles. There is a remnant who fear God, amidst many calamities, we enjoy many blessings; we have reason to sing of judgment and of mercy. Let us offer praise for what we enjoy; let us deprecate the evils which we either dread or feel; let us cease to do evil and learn to do well, then tho' God has been angry with us, his anger will turn away from us, and he will comfort us. (Muir 1798)

Some fifty of his discourses survive, including "The Virtuous Woman," which appeared in the new nation's first collection of sermons by Americans, *The American Preacher*, edited by David Austin (1791-93), part of the initial wave of nationalistic publishing that included Robert Aitken's Bible (1781-82), Noah Webster's *Elementary Spelling Book* (1783), Rev. Jedidiah Morse's *American Geography* (1789), and Amelia Simmons's *American Cookery* (1796). He published numerous items beyond discourses as well. His books include *Sermons* (Muir 1787), *An Examination of the Principles Contained in [Paine's] "The Age of Reason" in Ten Discourses* (Muir 1795, Stauffer 1918, Smylie 1972-73), and *Ten Sermons* (Muir 1812). He authored pronouncements on behalf of several governing bodies of the Presbyterian Church – two on behalf of the General Assembly, one addressing slavery both in general and specifically with regard to living in harmony within congregations that include both members who own slaves and members who consider ownership of slaves to be sinful (Muir 1795), and one on the expectations of a Christian life (Muir 1799). He also prepared a pronouncement on behalf of the Presbytery of Baltimore on "various duties [for parents], but especially on the religious education of their youth" (Muir 1811), and histories of the Presbytery of Baltimore and of the Meeting House congregation for a more comprehensive history of the Presbyterian Church in the United States (Muir 1804 and 1794).

Rev. Muir even published his expectations for members of his own congregation in leading a Christian life (Muir 1793). Several addresses to local groups survive – comments at the placing of the first cornerstone of the boundary of the newly created District of Columbia (Muir 1791), when the United States was at war and when peace was restored (Muir 1814 and 1815), and when the Bible Society of the District of Columbia was created (Muir 1814).

Two of his published discourses are closely associated with George Washington – the one he delivered at a service for the National Day of Solemn Humiliation, Fasting, and Prayer, attended by Washington in 1798 previously cited (Muir 1798, Nash 1965), and those that he delivered to memorialize George Washington following Washington's death in December 1799 (Muir 1800) and at the National Day of Mourning that closed the formal period of mourning on the twenty-second of February 1800 (Muir 1800, McGroarty 1932, Boller 1961, Kahler 2008). He also edited a religious periodical, *The Monthly Visitant; or, Something Old*, which was printed by Samuel Snowden and distributed from Alexandria. As with most such periodicals, it was short-lived and survived for only six 40-page issues during 1816. Copies of all of his works known to exist are held by the Meeting House Archive.

Rev. Muir's distinguished ministry was recognized by Yale College with an honorary Doctor of Divinity (D.D.) in 1791. He delivered his final sermon on the last Lord's Day of May 1820. On the eighth of August 1820, he died and was buried beneath the pulpit of the Meeting House. His wife, Elizabeth, and their three daughters and one son survived him. The memorial placed in the Meeting House near the original pulpit describes him as "Amiable and unobtrusive in his manners, kind and benevolent in his disposition, diligent and unwearied in the discharge of his pastoral duties. He died as he lived, an illustrious example of that faith 'once delivered to the saints'."

3. The Original Diary and Its Transcription

Throughout 1805 the Rev. Dr. James Muir made diary entries on the pages left blank for this purpose in the *Town and Country Almanac for the Year of Our Lord, 1805*.... It had been printed and published in Alexandria by the firm of Robert and John Gray (Robert Gray was a member of the Meeting House congregation). The original almanac-diary is now held by the Library of Virginia in Richmond, Virginia, the governmental archive of the Commonwealth of Virginia. The original document is retained in Special Collections – call number AY326.A3 T71; and a photostatic copy resides in the Personal Papers Collection of Archives Research Services – call number 25345. A photocopy of the original document is in the Muir Collection of the Meeting House Archive.

The original *Town and Country Almanac* volume measures a handy 7 by 4 inches. Almanacs were staples of American printers during the eighteenth and early nineteenth centuries. They typically included a day-by-day calendar with daily weather predicttions, astronomical information, and a variety of short written pieces meant to entertain, plus space for maintaining a diary (Stowell 1977). One of these early almanacs, the *Farmer's Almanac*, first published in Dublin, New Hampshire in 1792, continues to be issued annually as the *Old Farmer's Almanac*. It is the oldest continuously published periodical in America.

No doubt Rev. Muir recorded daily events in almanac-diaries during other years as well, but the one produced by Robert and John Gray in 1805 is the only one known to survive. While the printing partnership of Robert and John Gray had existed for several years, it dissolved during 1805. At least one other Alexandria printing firm, that of Peter Cottom and James A. Stewart, published almanacs for many years. Rev. Muir's 1805 almanac-diary consists of eighty-nine pages, excluding the blank pages at both front and rear. Thirty-four of these pages include explicitly almanac-related material and "selections, instructive and entertaining, in prose and verse." Fifty-three of the almanac's pages include handwritten entries by the Rev. Muir.

The main body of the almanac consists of sets of pages with a repeating pattern of contents – an almanac page, followed by several blank pages for maintaining a diary, and a second almanac page. The cycle repeats itself for each calendar month. Each initial page in the cycle, devoted to almanac material, lists each day of the month with its "Judgment of weather", e.g., "very cold," "fine," or "rain," the times of sunrise and sunset, and several miscellaneous pieces of information. Diary pages follow the initial almanac page – four pages left blank for making hand-written entries (Figure 2). The second almanac page, which rounds out the cycle, lists additional information for the same month as the initial almanac page, including phases of the moon, locations of the "most conspicuous planets and fixed stars," and a few other items.

The transcription of the diary presented here contains all of the handwritten entries that appear in the original work, less notes made by the Rev. Muir on pages with the month by month calendar and almanac entries, and entries that are indecipherable (noted by "___"). The relatively few hand-written entries that appear in the calendar and almanac pages include Muir's own empirical weather observations placed atop the printed predicted conditions provided by the almanac, e.g., the almanac's printed "Judgment of Weather" for the second of March is "cold" over which Rev. Muir entered the word "mild," and the printed weather for the ninth of March is "windy" and Rev. Muir entered "warm."

The transcription also omits material from the publisher-furnished almanac and literary entries. The original volume did not contain page numbers. Page numbers were added by hand at an unknown date and are located at the bottom gutter side of each page. Material that has been added to diary entries appears in brackets, i.e., "[ ]." Indecipherable material is indicated with spaces and an underscore, i.e., "___."

Monetary values are expressed in terms of dollars, pounds and shillings per the original diary. Money from many nations continued to circulate in Virginia in 1805 – a table at the rear of the almanac lists the values of twenty-four different foreign coins in terms of U.S. dollars, cents (hundredths of a dollar), and thousandths of a dollar.

Rev. Muir's spelling practices have been retained, but current forms of punctuation have been added for clarity. Text appearing in the transcription that is not original to the diary, which consists mostly of annotations that follow Rev. Muir's passages, are presented in italics. These annotations are expressed in the histor-

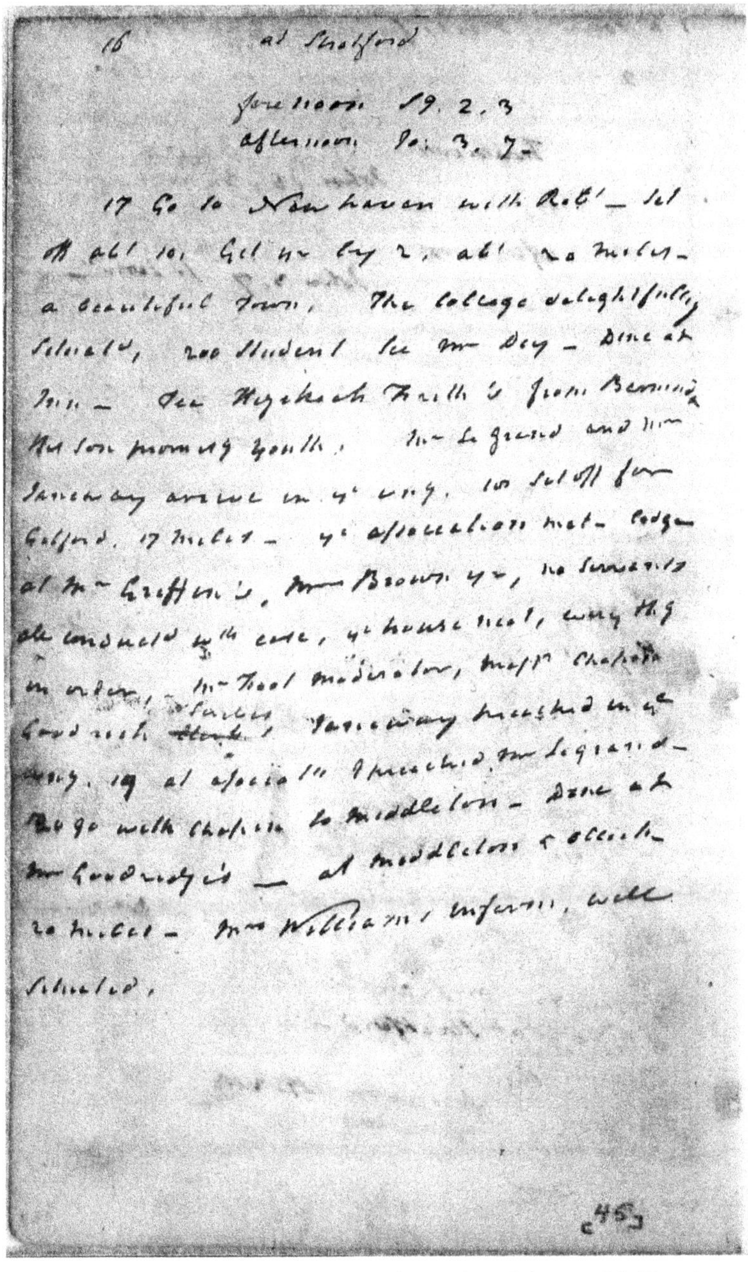

Figure 2. Page of Rev. Dr. Muir's 1805 Diary with Entries for 16 to 19 June (slightly reduced from original).

ic present tense in an attempt to assist the reader to mentally dwell in 1805.

Part II. THE REV. DR. JAMES MUIR'S DIARY

1st [January]

Dine at Mr. S[amuel] Craig's with the Rev. Mr. Samuel Wood. [Attend meeting of the Church] Committee [that convenes] in the evening; four [members are] present. A stormy night. Tarry at Mr. [John] Hunter's.

Notes: Samuel and Joanna Craig are members of Rev. Muir's congregation. The second dinner guest of the Craig household is probably the Rev. Dr. Samuel Wood (1752-1836), visiting from New England. Rev. Wood is a well-known educator and clergyman affiliated with both the Presbyterian and Congregational denominations.

The Church Committee is the body within a Presbyterian congregation that is responsible for its temporal (worldly) affairs, such as finances and property maintenance; the Session, composed of Elders and the minister, is responsible for the spiritual well-being of the congregation.

John Hunter (1760-1826), originally from Ayrshire, Scotland, as is Rev. Muir, is an Alexandria shipbuilder whose yard is located at the foot of Wilkes Street. He and his wife, Cordelia Meeks Hatton Hunter, are members of the Meeting House congregation, and he serves the congregation as a member of the Church Committee. Perhaps Rev. Muir's tarrying means he spent the "stormy night" following the Church Committee meeting at the Hunter home.

6th [January, a Sunday]

Forenoon Luke 13, 6-10.
Afternoon 2 Pet[er] 1, 16. 1st clauses. 1st sermon [he delivers on this passage].
Heb[rew] 1, 1. 1st sermon [he delivers on this passage].
Very severe weather. This [is the] week the river shut up.
The Seconds of [Aaron] Burr and [Alexander] Hamilton on the fatal Duel, found guilty. The punishment [is] Dis[en]franchised for 20 years excluded from all rights claimed by citizens.

Notes: The Potomac River becoming "shut up," i.e., frozen solid and therefore closed to shipping, is an event of particular importance in a port town such as Alexandria. It means that the most important activity of the local economy has ceased to function. Rev. Muir will make reference to river conditions again ten days later, on January 18 (Miller 1992, Shomette 2003).

The severity of the winter of 1805 is noted in the local newspaper come April – "The present winter, since a few days before Christmas, has been one of the most severe experienced for a great many years back... There is at present about seven feet of snow in the woods where it does not drift. The usual quantity about the middle of March, when it is generally at the highest, is from four to five feet." (Alexandria Daily Advertiser 3 April 1805 p. 3). Anne Riston, who spends a winter in Alexandria during this period, responds poetically to such conditions – "As there had been a fall of snow, Followed by a frost, intense and cold, Which did in icy bondage hold, The river, and the harbour o'er, As if it meant to break no more; The whole appeared a plate of glass, A large extended frozen mass." (Riston 1809).

The "seconds of Aaron Burr and Alexander Hamilton" are Nathaniel Pendleton and William Van Hess. They had served as seconds in the duel in which Burr killed Hamilton at Weehawken, New Jersey, across the Hudson River from New York City on the 11th of July 1804.

Rev. Muir does not record that he performs a marriage service on Thursday of this week (10 January) for Amos Alexander (1770-1826) and Elizabeth Wroe, members of his congregation. Amos Alexander had previously served as Mayor of Alexandria and would become a director of the Franklin Bank and of the soon-to-be-constructed Alexandria and Leesburg Turnpike.

13[th] [January, a Sunday]

Forenoon 2 Pet[er] 1, 16. 2nd ser[mo]n [on this passage].

"Do thyself no harm." ["But Paul cried out with a loud voice, saying, 'Do thyself no harm, for we are all here." Acts 16:28].

Afternoon 1 Sam[ue]l 1, 17.18.

"Is any afflicted let him pray." ["Is any among you afflicted? let him pray. Is any merry? let him sing psalms." James 5:15]

Note: Rev. Muir's references here and elsewhere to a "1st sermon" or a "2nd sermon" is independent of delivery during the forenoon or afternoon services. It indicates that his discourse on *a Bible verse extends over more than a single sermon, or that he is addressing successive verses during successive services. The inclusion of excerpts from Biblical texts such as "Do thyself no harm" remains unclear. He unfailingly includes Biblical text references for his forenoon and afternoon sermons, so he may be simply recording passing thoughts or text references for the less formal evening service that he will lead later in the day.*

15th [January]

[Rev.] Mr. [William] Maffitt called upon me. [He is] in town with [his] daughter who is unwell. Pay him $12.50 due on Mollie's wages. Give him a check for $54 [for] the Bank Dividend. He gave me $12 to pay Mr. [Andrew] Jamieson an __ .
 I payed accordingly.

Notes: Rev. William Maffitt (1769-1828) is a Presbyterian minister and Rev. Muir's closest clerical colleague. He conducts a school at Chantilly, his estate in western Fairfax County, Virginia, and serves as a supply minister to several Presbyterian congregations in Northern Virginia. He had previously resided with the Muir family in Alexandria while heading the Alexandria Academy from 1793 to 1804 (Eaves 1936, McGroarty 1940b, Morrill 1987). When living in Alexandria, he also served as a trustee and director of the Alexandria Library Company; as chaplain of the Washington Society; and as moderator of the Presbytery of Baltimore. Following his marriage to Henrietta "Harriot" Turberville, widow of Richard Lee Turberville, in 1803, he resigned his position at the Alexandria Academy, and the new couple moved to the Chantilly estate (Anderson 1979). Rev. Muir's son, Samuel Crichton Muir, studies with Rev. Maffitt during 1805.

Mollie is one of several female servants in the employ of the Muir family during the year. Rev. Muir typically identifies them only by their Christian names in his diary. Other servants engaged by the Muirs during the year are Sarah, Sally, Betsy, Delly, and Molly Price. Arrangements with these servants other than the payments indicated in Rev. Muir's diary remain unknown. The Muirs previously had received at least one person into their household under contract with Alexandria's Overseers of the Poor "to learn the Art, Trade or Mystery of a house servant and after the manner of an apprentice..." (Indenture dated 19 July 1800 in Meeting House Archive).

Andrew Jamieson (1751-1825), originally from Scotland, emigrated to Alexandria during the 1780s. He established the Jamieson Bakery in 1785, which becomes famous for its biscuits, a form of cracker, and grows into one of Alexandria's largest businesses. Rev. Muir sends Jamieson crackers to several relatives during the year. Jamieson crackers receive attention from British troops when they sack Alexandria during the War of 1812, as well. Andrew's son, Robert, continues to operate the firm into the 1860s. Andrew Jamieson is active in Alexandria public life, serving as a trustee of Alexandria's Poor and Work House; an active member of the St. Andrew's Society; a charter member of the Alexandria Library Company; and on the 1803 Committee of Health during that year's yellow fever epidemic. He and his wife, Mary Sweet Jamieson (1769-1824), are members of the Meeting House congregation, and he serves the congregation as an elder and trustee (Bromberg 1999, Duncan 1823 Vol. 1, p. 287).

18th [January]
[Rev.] Mr. Maffitt returned with Sam[ue]l [Crichton Muir]. Sent him a pair of stockings. The [midweek evening prayer-worship service] meeting attend[ed] by 15.

Freez[in]g, river shut [to traffic].

Note: Samuel Crichton Muir (1789-1832) is the Rev. James and Elizabeth Muir's son. He is sixteen years of age and studying with the Rev. William Maffitt at Chantilly during the year. The diary notes that father and son exchange letters several times during the year. Samuel Muir will go on to receive training in medicine at the University of Edinburgh, and then serve as a medical officer in the U.S. Army. He succumbs to cholera while treating victims during the Black Hawk War in Illinois.

20th [January, a Sunday]
Forenoon Luke 7, 35–.

Afternoon attend funeral of Mrs. [Mary Ann] Faw. In a fit of lunacy [i.e., being of unsound mind, she] hanged herself by a handkerchief tied to the bed post & thrown over the __ with a stepping stone was found an hour after the fatal deed. "Lead us not [into] temptation but deliver us from evil." At the same time Mrs. [Margaret Smelt] Gadsby was buried at the Episcopal Church.

The weather extremely cold, [with] a snow storm, which occasioned the omission of service in the afternoon. The __ .

Notes: Margaret Smelt Gadsby is the first wife of John Gadsby, owner of Gadsby's Tavern. Gadsby's Tavern, at the southwest corner of North Royal and Cameron streets, is one of Alexandria's major inns and a famous gathering place (it operates today as a restaurant and museum.)

Rev. Muir conducts the memorial service for Mary Ann Faw (1770-1805). She is interred in the Burial Ground at the Meeting House. Her husband, Abraham Faw, is the town coroner and a justice of the peace. The Burial Ground at the Meeting House will receive burials for another four years, until the Presbyterian Cemetery, a mile west of the Meeting House, is established in 1809 (Van Horn 2009).

23rd [January]

[Rev.] Mr. [William] Maffitt in town. Dine with him at Mr. Ch[arles] Lee's. No [midweek prayer-worship] meeting in the evening.

Received a very friendly card from James S. Scott, begging my acceptance of a Suit of Clothes – Pantaloons of cotton velvet, silk vest, coat of tweed cloth. He speaks of <u>Duty</u> be[in]g __ the measure, of doing something for the aid [of those] who by [their] calling __ are prevented from engage[in]g in worldly pursuits. Acknowledged [the gift] on the 24th. His card __ home __ .

The day thaws. __ in the even[in]g & during the night. Clear on 25th __ thaws. W[inds are from the] south. Mostly fog. Frost towards morning of 26th, but cloudy wet evening.

Notes: Charles Lee (1758-1815), a graduate of the College of New Jersey (Princeton University) and now a lawyer in Alexandria, had served as U.S. Attorney General during the administrations of George Washington and John Adams (from 1795 to 1801). He is a brother of Henry Lee, Richard Bland Lee, and Edmund Jennings Lee (Lee 1895).

James S. Scott is a cashier at Alexandria's Merchant's Bank. He and his wife, May Adgate Scott, who were married by Rev. Muir in 1802, are members of the Meeting House congregation.

27th [January, a Sunday]

Forenoon James 4, 8.

No sermon in the afternoon, the weather being snowy. __ the ground covered with snow. N[orth]W[est wind].

28th [January]

An order was presented me from W[illia]m W. Newbold to pay Capt. Jo[hn] Tucker 5£ 6sh -p (British Currency) –

Mary Stewart's passage in June past from Bermuda to Norfolk	16$
Mary [Muir] d[itt]o	12$
	28$

Accepted the order.

Notes: Captain John Tucker, originally from Bermuda, is a local Alexandria merchant in the import-export trade, with a pier and warehouse at the foot of King Street. His family from Bermuda visits the Muir household in August. Presumably, Rev. Muir paid the bill that was issued in British currency in U.S. dollars.

Mary Wardlaw Muir (1794-1860), eleven years of age, is the family's second daughter. She spends a portion of the year in Bermuda. It is at least the second time she has lived there for a spell, perhaps a school term, with the Welman family. She was spending time in Bermuda when Oliver Deming Welman, Rev. Muir's brother in law, died in 1802.

Mary Stewart is the daughter of one of two Stewart families in the Meeting House congregation, either John Ainsworth Stewart and his wife, Elizabeth Dunlap Stewart, or James A. Stewart and his wife, Jane Stewart. John and James Stewart are both local merchants. James Stewart is also a partner with Peter Cottom in the printing firm of Cottom and Stewart.

29th [January]

Purchase a coffee-mill $2 & tea $2.

3rd [February, a Sunday]

Forenoon   Jo[hn] 8, 47–.
Afternoon 1 Cor[inthians] 7, 29.30.31.

The weather extremely cold, N[orth]W[est] wind, and the wind strong [and] piercing.

4th [February]

Judge [Samuel] Chase's trial commenced. Gave a hot defence, read by himself. [Robert Goodloe] Harper, [Luther] Martin, and [Joseph] Hopkinson [serve as] his council.

*Notes: In this entry and in several that follow, Rev. Muir responds to the impeachment trial of U.S. Supreme Court Associate Justice Samuel Chase (1741-1811). Samuel Chase is not to be confused with Salmon Portland Chase (1808-1873) who will serve as U.S. Supreme Court Chief Justice from 1864 to 1873 (Rehnquist 1992). Justice Chase's trial is being conducted by the U.S. Senate. Chase, who had served on the Supreme Court since 1796, is a strong Federalist whose opinions, expressed from the bench in several highly politicized trials, have been found inappropriate by some. Impeachment proceedings in the U.S. House of Representatives, where the then-Republicans (anti-Federalists) hold a majority, are being led by John Randolph of Virginia. The House brought eight articles of impeachment against Justice Chase (see diary entry at 10 February). In his Senate trial, Chase will be acquitted on all eight charges, based primarily upon the defense that his actions were not crimes. He will continue to serve on the Supreme Court until his death in 1811. Local newspapers carry numerous articles on the proceedings (*Alexandria Daily Advertiser *31 January 1805 p. 3, 7 February 1805 p. 3, 16 February 1805 p. 2-3, 20 February 1805 p. 2-3, 4 March 1805 p. 3).*

Robert Goodloe Harper (1765-1825), a graduate of the College of New Jersey (Princeton University) and now a lawyer and resident of Baltimore, had previously served in the U.S. House of Representatives from South Carolina, and would later represent Maryland in the U.S. Senate. He is a member of Alexandria's Washington Society and will address that group's fundraising event for the Alexandria Academy in February 1810.

Luther Martin (1748-1826), another graduate of the College of New Jersey and a well-known trial lawyer, serves for decades as Attorney General of the State of Maryland.

Joseph Hopkinson (1770-1842) is a lawyer from Philadelphia who later serves in the U.S. House of Representatives.

6th [February]

Sarah, a white woman, came to be with us at 3$ a-month.

Note: Sarah is one of several female servants employed by the Muir family during the year.

8th [February]

Wrote the Rev. William Williamson [of] Leesburgh [now Leesburg, Virginia]. Mr. R__ promised to give [the letter to] Mr. Clifford to forward [to Rev. Williamson], invit[in]g [Rev.] Mr. W[illiam] Williamson [to join our congregation] at our [Lord's Supper] Sacrament, on the last Lord's day of March.

Notes: Information on Rev. Williamson is in notes at page 92.

Mr. Clifford is either Jeremiah Clifford or Nehemiah Clifford, both local Alexandria merchants. On the 21st of November, Rev. Muir will perform the burial service for Mrs. Clifford, whom he identifies only as "belonging to another denomination."

10th [February, a Sunday]

Forenoon Ps[alm] 107, 43.
Afternoon Luke 20, 27-39. 1st sermon [on this passage].

The weather mild. The snow begins to thaw, but the walking bad.

[In the following table, Rev. Muir records the results of voting in the U.S. Senate on the eight charges brought against Supreme Court Associate Justice Samuel Chase .]

Charges	Judge Chase's acquittal	Guilty	Not
1	Trial, of [John] Fries	16	18
2	Trial John Thompson Callender over-ruled objections of jury	10	24
3	Did not admit evidence John Taylor	18	16
4	Manifested injustice particularly intemperance	18	16
5	Awarding a capias against Callender illegal	[0]	34
6	Adjudging Callender to be tried at the term illegal	4	30
7	His conduct at New Castle Delaware	10	24
8	Delivering at Baltimore, opinions, Indecent, Extra-judicial	19	15
		95	177

Not guilty on the whole. Majority ['not guilty' by roughly 2:1] 177 [not guilty]/95 [guilty].

Note: In the fifth charge, "capias" is shorthand for "capias ad respondendum" (seizing a person to force them to answer a charge).

17th [February, a Sunday]
Forenoon   Matthew 6, 13 first clauses.
Afternoon   Luke 20, 27-39. 2nd sermon [on this passage].

The weather for some days has been extremely cold. Wind [from] N[orth]W[est]. Catholic lottery [at] Baltimore near the $20,000 [mark], which belongs to the church.

Mr. Ch[arles] Lee engaged to assist Judge Chase's counsel.

Note: The Catholic lottery mentioned here is one then being conducted to raise money for the construction of the Roman Catholic cathedral at Baltimore, the first to be erected in the United States. Lotteries such as this are utilized frequently during the eighteenth and early nineteenth centuries to finance activities ranging from the construction of roads and canals to the building of libraries and places of worship. This particular lottery is promoted extensively in Alexandria's newspapers as "Catholic Cathedral Church Lottery" (see Alexandria Daily Advertiser, *2 January 1805 and subsequent dates). The cathedral, designed by Benjamin Henry Latrobe, will be under construction from the summer of 1806 until 1821.*

19th [February]
Received a letter from [Rev.] Mr. [William] Maffitt in w[hic]h [he] says "Samuel [Rev. Muir's son] now making greater improvement than he ever did since I knew him. He [Samuel] appears to be acquiring a fondness for eeling" wrote Mr. Maffitt.

Note: Eeling, the trapping of eels for eating, is a common practice in the Potomac River at this time.

20th [February]
B[e]g[in] an address promot[ing] religious feel[in]g for [bi-annual fund-raising program of Washington Society on] 22[nd].

*Note: Rev. Muir makes no record here, but he performs a marriage service for Moses Janney and Judith Lawrence of Massachusetts on the 21st of February (*Alexandria Daily Advertiser *21 February 1805).*

On the 22nd [the birth anniversary of George Washington, I] attend orations of the Day [by] Wm. Douglass Simms, our [Washington Society] orator. He was collected and firm, the composition clear, yet sufficiently flowery, __ yet nervous. The specimen [i.e., the speech by Simms] promised future success [for him]. Dine with <u>Washington Society</u>. They presented Capt. [Lewis] Nicholas with $31. Drank Punch at Dr. [Elisha Cullen] Dick's, whose daughter was married to Gideon Pearce, Esq. last even[in]g.

*Notes: William Douglass Simms (1783-1822), son of Revolutionary War veteran and Alexandria Mayor, Colonel Charles Simms (1755-1819), addresses Alexandria's Washington Society celebration of the birth of George Washington. Later in the year, the young Simms will announce that he "has commenced the practice of law" in local district courts (*Alexandria Daily Advertiser *26 August 2005 p. 4). The celebration of George Washington's birth anniversary is one of two fund-raising events conducted each year by the Washington Society in support of the endowment of the Free School, which is also known as the Washington School, a unit within the Alexandria Academy.*

The Washington Society was established in 1800 by Rev. Muir and other leading citizens of Alexandria to memorialize George Washington following his death in 1799, and to assist in providing continued financial support for free education in Alexandria, which had been initiated by a contribution from Washington and others in 1785. Public addresses are sponsored by the group twice a year, on the birth anniversary of George Washington in February and on the nation's Independence Day in July. These addresses are usually delivered at the Presbyterian Meeting House or the Episcopal Church. Over the years, addresses are presented by Francis Scott Key, George Washington Parke Custis, and John Marshall among many other luminaries of the day. The public address is preceded by a street procession from Market Square that includes children from the Washington Free School. Following the service, the group will again march through the streets to a local inn, such as Gadsby's Tavern, where members of the Society dine (McGroarty 1928, 1932, Whitton 1982, Alexandria Daily Advertiser *20 February 1805 p. 2).*

Lewis Nicholas, also "Lewis Nichola" (1717-1807) and with ranks ranging from Captain through General, is a native of Ireland who had served in the Revolutionary War and is now a resident of Alexandria. During the Revolutionary War, he formed a Regiment of Invalids and published A Treatise of Military Exercise, Calculated for the Use of Americans, In Which Every Thing That is Supposed Can Be of Use to Them is Retained, and Such

Manoeuvres As Are Only for Show and Parade Omitted; To Which is Added Some Directions on the Other Points of Discipline *(Philadelphia: Styner and Cist, 1776)*. *An original member of the Society of the Cincinnati, he is buried in the Meeting House Burial Ground.*

The $31 raised in donations provides financial support for the Alexandria Academy.

Elisha Cullen Dick (1762-1825), a local physician who also runs a pharmacy and serves as the Mayor during 1805, was one of the three attending physicians to George Washington at his death in 1799. He maintains residences in town and at Cottage Hill in Fairfax County. He had originally studied to enter the Presbyterian clergy but was never ordained. He is a member of the Meeting House congregation until 1812, when he becomes a strong anti-slavery advocate and joins the Alexandria Friends Meeting (Quakers).

Julia Dick, Elisha Cullen Dick's only daughter, and Gideon Pearce, Esq., a wealthy landowner from Kent County, Maryland, were married the previous evening. Their son, James Alfred Pearce (1805-1862), will attend the Alexandria Academy and become a member of the U.S. House of Representatives and U.S. Senate from the State of Maryland.

24th [February, a Sunday]
Forenoon M[atth]ew 13, 24-31.
Afternoon Psalm 110, 3 final clause. 1st sermon [on
                                          this passage].

Note: Rev. Muir makes no record in this portion of his diary, but he performs marriage ceremonies for George Bowling and Elizabeth Veitch and for Andrew Lyon and Mary Massey on the 26th of February (Brumbaugh 1918-20). Andrew Lyon is a blacksmith with a shop on the waterfront.

28th [February]
Weather has been wet [and] disagreeable. Confined for two days with a cold. Attended [midweek service the previous evening] with a cold, which affected my breast.

1st [March]
Judge Chase acquitted very honourably. One third of the Senate sufficient to acquit. In one article unanimously acquitted. In

others [he was acquitted] by more than two thirds – 15 [senators] was the lowest number he had [voting for acquittal], of which 19 [was what] would have acquitted, 34 b[ein]g the number [of members] in Senate.

Note: Rev. Muir once again makes reference to the impeachment trial of U.S. Supreme Court Associate Justice Samuel Chase then underway in the U.S. Senate. The verdict is announced this day.

3rd [March, a Sunday]
 Forenoon M[atthe]w 28, 18.19.20. 1st sermon [on this passage].
 Afternoon P[salm] 110, 3. 2nd sermon [on this passage].

Council [members elected from Alexandria's four wards.]
No. 1. A[aron] Hewes, W[illiam] Harper, J[acob] Hoffman, Al[exander] Smith
No. 2. J[onah] Thompson, J[ohn] Lumsdon, H[enry] Rose, M[atthew] Sexsmith
No. 3. [John] McKinney, Jon[athan] Swift, E[dmund] J[ennings] Lee, G[eorge] Deneale
No. 4. M[atthew] Robinson, J[ohn] Cohagan, R[obert] Young, J[ohn] Janney
 [Jonah] <u>Thompson</u> Mayor, Walter Jones __ in place.

Notes: This is the second election for local officials since Alexandria's government was re-chartered the previous year within the District of Columbia. Election results are reported in the Alexandria Daily Advertiser *on Wednesday (6 March 1805 p. 3). Council members William Harper, Alexander Smith, Henry Rose (also chosen president of the Council), John McKinney, Jonathan Swift, George Deneale, and Robert Young, and Mayor Jonah Thompson, are members of Rev. Muir's congregation.*

Thomas Jefferson is sworn into office for a second term as President of the United States in Washington, D.C. on Monday, the 4th of March.

7th [March]
Received a letter from [Rev.] Mr. [James] Inglis, which I answered, and put in the post office engaging to assist him at the Sacrament [of the Lord's Supper] on 7th April.
 Today payed Wm. Cowery 5$ for Mary [Muir] in full until 10th Instant. __ general by __ 6$ in full for her 1st quarter, 6$ having been payed at her entering, __ percent __ 5th.

Jonah Thompson, Esq. chosen mayor.

Notes: Rev. Dr. James Inglis (1777-1820) serves the First Presbyterian Church at Baltimore.

Jonah Thompson (1758-1834) is a local landowner, merchant, justice of the peace, President of the Bank of Alexandria, and the newly elected Mayor. He and his wife, Martha Peyton Thompson, who reside at 211 North Fairfax Street, are both members of the Meeting House congregation. Newspaper accounts of the recent election indicate that re-voting was required in Ward Two, so the reporting of election results was delayed.

10th [March, a Sunday]
Forenoon Matthew 28, 18.19.20. 2nd sermon [on this passage].
Afternoon Acts 3, 22 and Heb[rews] 12, 25.

Mr. [Philip] Fendall died this morning. [He was] in usual health last Lord's day and at church [service]. Taken ill on Monday.

11th [March]
Attend his funeral, [he was] 70 years old.

Note: Philip Richard Fendall (1734-1805), a local entrepreneur, banker, and attorney, who resided at 614 Oronoco Street (today known as Lee-Fendall House).

12th [March]
Take 7 oz. cream [of] tartar, some __, some oats. A box segars [cigars] 3$ Mr. L__. Directed Mr. Norburgh, who is gone to New York [City], to pay Robt. Welman $5.50/100 for a box of segars [cigars] sent me.

Note: Rev. Muir makes no record in this portion of his diary, but he performs a marriage service for Frederick Shuck and Elizabeth Bogan on the 14th of March (Brumbaugh 1918-20).

15th [March]
Received from Mr. Hartshorne one Bush[e]l of meal 7 [shillings]/__.

Note: William Hartshorne (unknown-1816), a local merchant, landowner, and Quaker, engages in business with several members of the Meeting House congregation. He resides two blocks from the parsonage on Wilkes Street, between Royal and Pitt streets.

17th [March, a Sunday]
Forenoon   Luke 7, 11-19.
Afternoon   Philip[p]ians 2, 8.

The forenoon a funeral Sermon for Elizabeth McKay, sister of Mrs. [Eliza] Black's, aged 19 y[ears]. [She] had languished 10 years under a cancer. Mr. [Josiah Hewes] Davis being sick. The church crowded.

Notes: Eliza Black is the wife of David Black, a ship's captain with a store at the corner of King and Washington streets. They reside on Pitt Street and are members of the Meeting House congregation.

Josiah Hewes Davis (1783-1862) is a ship's chandler (supplier). He and his wife, Sarah M. Davis, are members of the Meeting House congregation, and he serves the congregation as a member of its Church Committee.

18th [March]
Received a letter from [Rev.] Mr. [William] Maffitt. Mrs. [Henrietta Turberville] M[affitt] had presented him a fine <u>daughter</u> on 16th & is on her way of recovering. Wrote [Rev.] Mr. Maffitt.

Wrote in the course of the week letters to [Rev.] Mr. [Stephen B.] Balch & [to Rev.] Mr. [Conrad] Spence inviting [them] to assist at the sacrament [of the Lord's Supper] with the Revd. Jo[hn] Glendy, and [to discuss] Presbytery business.

Notes: The "fine daughter" is Henrietta Maffitt, the daughter of Henrietta and William Maffitt. Rev. Muir baptizes her in April.

Rev. Dr. Stephen Bloomer Balch (1747-1833) serves the Bridge-Street (today's Georgetown) Presbyterian Church in the District of Columbia from 1780 to 1833. He is a close associate of Rev. Muir's in the Presbytery of Baltimore.

Rev. Conrad Spence is a Presbyterian minister who had been licensed to preach by the Presbytery of Hanover (Indiana) in 1803 and was installed the previous year at the congregation at Captain John (now Cabin John), Maryland at which Rev. Muir had presided.

Rev. Dr. John Glendy is a Presbyterian minister who will be installed as minister of Second Presbyterian Church at Baltimore with Rev. Muir presiding over the service (diary entry at 6 April).

Presbyteries are the local governing body in the Presbyterian Church. The Meeting House congregation is a member of the Presbytery of Baltimore during this period.

24th [March, a Sunday]
Forenoon Matthew 28, 18.19.20. 3rd sermon [on this passage].
Afternoon Philippians 2, 9.10.11. N[orth wind].
Mr. [Josiah Hewes] Davis still sick. Many of the congregat[io]n with us [at worship in spite of the weather].

25th [March]
Receiv[e]d letter from the Revd. William Williamson, his engagements prevent him from b[ein]g with us at the sacrament [of the Lord's Supper on the 31st of March]. Will enlist him on a further occasion. It will give him pleasure. The Presb[yter]y [of] Winchester meets at Leesburgh [Leesburg] on 11th April.

The Letter['s postage] p[ai]d.

26th [March]
[Rev.] Mr. [John] Boggs in Town.

Note: Rev. John Boggs (1780-post 1851), who had been licensed to preach by the Presbytery of Winchester a year earlier, was assigned by the Presbyterian Church's Synod of Virginia as an itinerant "principally in the northern neck of Virginia... [where] in most places he was cordially received, and in some his preaching was attended with very hopeful appearances" (Presbyterian Church 1827 p. 323). He subsequently serves congregations in Virginia's Shenandoah Valley, and after 1807 from South Carolina to Ohio. During this visit to Alexandria, he preaches at the Meeting House at least three times, beginning on Tuesday and climaxing on Sunday with a service that includes the Lord's Supper.

Although the sermons he delivers at the Meeting House do not survive, his presence in the pulpit here represents an example of the "reasonable revivalism" that prevails within urban Presbyterian congregations during this period – a style of evangelism characterized by decorum, reasoned argumentation, and solemnity, which attempts to appeal to educated urban audiences (Thomas 1983). The Rev. Muir, who sought spiritual revival among the members of his community, did not adopt the more explicitly emotional methods often employed throughout rural areas and in some urban communities, including Alexandria during this period by local Methodists, whose "considerable revival" during these very years brings several hundred new members to the Alexandria Methodist congregation (Watters 1806, Stukenbroeker 1974).

27th [March]
[Rev.] Mr. [John] Boggs at [midweek evening prayer-worship] meet[in]g. About 30 Present.

28th [March]
Wet day.

30th [March]
[Rev.] Mr. [John] Boggs still here at the meet[in]g [at] Ch[urch]. Wet day. Most of our communicants present [for this Saturday service].

31st [March, a Sunday]
Forenoon Acts 11, 26. "The Disciples were called <u>Christians</u> first at Antioch" Action Sermon [preceding Lord's Supper].

The preceding day being wet, and this morning [also], the assembly not full but respectable, ab[out] 36 communicants. Raise a collection for the use of the Presbytery of Baltimore – 24$ 25/100.

Afternoon [Rev.] Mr. [John] Boggs preached. "The eyes of the Lord are every where beholding the good & the evil!" [Proverbs 15:3] He had been reading __ from which he had taken many parts. Wrote the Revd. Mr. W[illiam] Williamson in answer to his [letter, and] send [it] by [Rev.] Mr. Boggs.

Note: "Action Sermon" is the term commonly used by Scottish Presbyterians for the sermon preceding the service of the Lord's Supper (the "action"). March is one of the four months of the year when the Lord's Supper is commonly served among Presbyterian congregations during this period, the others being June, September, and December.

2nd [April]

Meet [with] the [Church] Committee [of the Meeting House]. Full quorum [present] at Mr. [Jonathan] Swift's [home].

Note: Jonathan Swift (unknown-1824), originally from Massachusetts, is a local merchant; consular agent representing the governments of Denmark and Sweden; president of the board of trustees of Alexandria's Poor and Work House; and treasurer of the Washington Society. The Swift residence, Colross, is located in the 1100-block of Oronoco Street. It will be dismantled and relocated to Princeton, New Jersey in 1927, and eventually incorporated into the facilities of the Princeton Day School. Rev. Muir will spend his final days at Colross in August 1820. Jonathan Swift's wife, Ann Foster Roberdeau Swift, is the daughter of General Daniel Roberdeau. They are both members of the Meeting House congregation.

3rd [April]
Set off for Baltimore [Maryland]. Leave Alex[andria] about 10 [in the] morn[in]g. [Leave] Georgetown 10 [in the] evening. On road all night. At Baltimore about 10 [on] morning [of the next day].

Note: Rev. Muir travels to Baltimore for several purposes – to attend a meeting of the Presbytery of Baltimore; to participate in the installation of a minister at Baltimore's newly formed Second Presbyterian Church; to preach on the Lord's Day at First Presbyterian Church; and to visit friends. He is away from Alexandria for seven days – a day in transit each way and five days at Baltimore. Among other actions taken at the sessions of presbytery is the passing of a resolution that condemns dueling "after considerable debate" (Presbytery of Baltimore 5 April 1805).

Later in the year, action on dueling by the General Assembly of the Presbyterian Church is reported in the local newspaper – resolved "unanimously, to discountenance [dueling] on all occasions, and to recommend to all its ministers to refuse to attend a funeral of any person killed in a duel, and to admit no person giving or accepting a challenge the privileges of the church" (Alexandria Daily Advertiser 24 September 1805 p. 3).

Rev. Muir's diary includes entries relating to two contemporary duels. One is between Aaron Burr and Alexander Hamilton, which had occurred in July of the previous year (diary entry at 11 January). The other is between Enoch M. Lyles of

Alexandria and John F. Bowie of Maryland (diary entry at 7 August).

4th [April]
Lodging [in Baltimore with] Mr. [Christopher] Johnston.

Note: Christopher Johnston (1750-1819), originally from Scotland, is a Baltimore merchant; member of the town's Common Council; and elder of the First Presbyterian Church at Baltimore.

5th [April]
Preach before Presbytery [of Baltimore, at First Presbyterian Church] from M[atthe]w 28, 20 [to] last clause – "I am with you always." [Rev.] Mr. [John] Glendy chosen moderator [of Presbytery]. [Rev.] Mr. [Conrad] Spence [chosen] clerk.

Dine in the family way with [Rev.] Mr. [James] Inglis [who] had been at the Presby[ter]y in the morning. Saw George N__.

Note: Among other business conducted on its first day of sessions, presbytery considers changes to the Presbyterian Church's "Form of Government," which had been recommended by the 1804 General Assembly of the church; the supply of clergy to small congregations; and a resolution concerning dueling, namely "The Presbytery of Baltimore considering the alarming progress of the detestable spirit & practice of dueling in this country, convinced that as the spirit & practice of dueling are supported by Publick opinion they ought to be combated by direct influence on Publick opinion tending to render infamous that which in this case is impiously accounted honourable, & believing that a Publick & solemn expression, & especially a practical one, of abhorrence & opposition to this murderous system of false honour, unitedly (sic) & particularly made by the clergy of our church would under the blessing of heaven go far towards its suppression, Resolved, that the commissioners of this Presbytery to the next General Assembly be instructed to use their endeavours to obtain the passing of a resolution by that venerable body enjoining it upon the clergy of the Presbyterian Church in the U. S. of America, that they scrupulously refuse to join to render any kind of funeral honours to an person who has fallen in a Duel, or is known to have fought a Duel, or to have given, or accepted a Challenge for that purpose." This resolution, "after considerable debate, was taken on the whole, and is passed in the affirmative" (Presbytery of Baltimore 5 April 1805).

6th [April]
Preside at Installation [of the Rev.] Mr. [John] Glendy. Gave Charge to the minister, [and to the] people [members of the congregation]. Dine at Mr. [George] Salmon's.
Presby[tery] in session until 9 at night.

Notes: Rev. John Glendy is installed as the minister of Baltimore's newly established Second Presbyterian Church, whose creation had been initiated by the First Presbyterian Church in 1803 (Smith 1899).

George Salmon (unknown-1807) is President of the Bank of Baltimore and an elder and member of the Church Committee of the First Presbyterian Church at Baltimore.

7th [April, a Sunday, at First Presbyterian Church, Baltimore]
Forenoon   Preach Acts 11, 26.
  [Rev.] Mr. [James] Inglis fenc[e]d Table [for service of the
  Lord's Supper]. [I] offered consecration Prayer. [Rev.] Mr.
  [Stephen B.] Balch exhorted. Service ended [with] a profes-
  ion of faith; mean grace, seal[ed] covenant, great attention
  & seriousness.
[Rev.] Mr. [Conrad] Spence preached in the afternoon.

Note: Rev. Conrad Spence, who had served the Cabin John Presbyterian congregation during the past year, had that relationship dissolved at the presbytery meeting at Baltimore just concluded – he was "dismissed, with an ample testimonial as to his reputation, and standing with this Presbytery" (Presbytery of Baltimore 5 April 1805).

8th [April]
[Remaining in Baltimore, I] Called upon Mr. Allison. I dine at Dr. [James] McHenry. T__ .
 [With] 15$ [I] purchased 3 tickets [for the] market-lottery.

Notes: Mr. Allison is perhaps a relative of the late Rev. Dr. Patrick Allison (1740-1802), who had been a friend of Rev. Muir's during his many years of service at Baltimore's First Presbyterian Church (Smith 1899).

James McHenry (1753-1816), originally from Ireland, had trained to become a doctor with Dr. Benjamin Rush at Philadelphia, and is now practicing in Baltimore. He had served in the Revolutionary War and as Secretary of War for Presidents Washington and Adams. He is a member of the First Presbyterian Church at Baltimore. Baltimore's Fort McHenry, which becomes famous when Francis Scott Key notices that its "star-spangled banner" continues to fly following bombardment during the War of 1812, is named for him.

9th [April]
[I] returned safe to Alex[andri]a.

10th [April]
Hear of Mrs. [Henrietta Turberville] Maffitt's leg [having been] struck with palsy.

11th [April]
Informed of Mrs. [Henrietta Turberville] Maffitt's death that morning. Set off at 4 p.m. for Chantilly, where I arrived ab[out] 9 p.m.

Note: The Maffitt family estate, Chantilly, is located in western Fairfax County, Virginia. It takes Rev. Muir five hours to travel the 30-40 miles of dirt roads between the Meeting House parsonage on Royal Street in Alexandria and Chantilly. The Little River Turnpike (now Duke Street, Virginia State Route 236, and U.S. Route 50), Northern Virginia's first publicly-subscribed highway improvement project, will connect Alexandria with Chantilly, and eventually Winchester in the Shenandoah Valley in a few years, but has yet to be completed.

12th [April]
Officiate at funeral [of Henrietta Turberville Maffitt].

Note: The 12th of April is also Rev. Muir's forty-eighth birthday.

13th [April]
Return to Alex[andri]a. Letters [received] from Messrs. C[hristopher] Johnston & Robert Oliver of Baltimore, & J[ame]s Chaplain of Bermuda, where Miss [Mary] Stewart is gone to School & can't be sent at present to America.

Notes: Robert Oliver (1757-1834), originally from Ireland, is a Baltimore merchant prince, who becomes a millionaire and director of the Baltimore and Ohio Railroad (Olson 1980). He is a member of First Presbyterian Church at Baltimore.

Christopher Johnston is another Baltimore businessman.

14th [April, a Sunday]

Forenoon 2 Cor[inthians] 5, 14.15 & 1 Tim[othy] 3, 16.
Baptize in church [the Meeting House] Mr. Robt. Young's daughter [Elizabeth Mary Young].
Afternoon Numbers 6, 22.23.24.25.26.27 [First portion of sermon on this passage] & 2 Cor[inthians] 13, 13.
Marry a couple [John Dixon and Mary Jura or Jerro] in the evening.

Notes: This is Easter Sunday, and as is normal among Presbyterians generally during this period, it is not celebrated at the Meeting House as the Lord's Day of Resurrection (Melton 1967, Thompson 1963-73, Rhys 1982, Nelson 2001). The texts chosen by Rev. Muir for the day's sermons are from Paul's letters to the Corinthians and Timothy in the New Testament – on living in faith as a Christian, and from Numbers in the Old Testament – citing the offerings to God by the leaders of the Israelites.

Elizabeth Mary Young (1804-1859) is a daughter of General Robert and Elizabeth Mary Conrad Young. She will be married to Richard Philip Fendall II (1794-1867) at the Meeting House in 1824 by Rev. Muir's successor, the Rev. Dr. Elias Harrison.

General Young (1768-1824) is a director of Alexandria's Bank of Potomac and President of the Mechanic's Bank. He had served as an officer in the Revolutionary War and will command the Second Brigade of the District of Columbia Militia in the War of 1812. He and his wife, Elizabeth Mary Conrad Young (1772-1810), reside at 1315 Duke Street. Both are members of the Meeting House congregation.

John Dixon is an Alexandria baker who later will become an inn keeper.

15th [April]

Answer the letters from Messrs. Christopher Johnston and Robert Oliver. [Engage in] presbytery office [work]. Rec'd Watson's Tracts.

Note: "Watson's Tracts" refers to Richard Watson's six-volume anthology, A Collection of Theological Tracts, *issued in London in 1791. Richard Watson (1737-1816) is the Regius Professor of Divinity in the University of Cambridge and Lord Bishop of Landaff. Among his numerous other works, Watson authored an attack on Thomas Paine –* An Antidote for Tom Paine's Theological and Political Poison: Containing, 1. Tom's Life, Interspersed with Remarks and Reflections, by P. Porcupine, 2. An Apology for the Bible, in a Series of Letters Addressed to Paine, by the Bishop of Landaff, 3. An Apology for Christianity, by the Same Learned, Elegant Writer, 4. An Answer to Paine's Anarchical Nonsense, Commonly Called the Rights of Man *(Philadelphia: William Cobbett, 1796).*

Rev. Muir had responded to Paine's Age of Reason *in a series of discourses that were published as* An Examination of the Principles Contained in "The Age of Reason" in Ten Discourses *(Muir 1795, Smylie 1972-73).*

16th [April]

Received from Mr. Jo[hn] Mills a present [of a] family Bible, London edition of the year [17]95, with superb Calf[skin binding] value[ed at] 20$. Read tracts. Made calls [visits].

[Rev.] Mr. [William] Maffitt received in town.

17th [April]

[Rev.] Mr. [Conrad] Spence [preaches] at [our] evening [midweek prayer-worship] meeting.

Baptize [Rev.] Mr. [William] Maffitt's daughter, Harriet, [who had been] b[orn] 16th March. Mrs. [Henrietta Turberville] Maffitt died 11th April.

20th [April]

Received a letter from Robt. Oliver [of] Baltimore of [the] 18th. He is willing to secure Miss [Mary] Stewart into his family at eight Dollars a month. Three white servants are in family, with which Miss S[tewart] must eat, [and] four Negroes. They go in a few weeks to the[ir] country [estate]. If Miss S[tewart] assents to his terms, he will let me know when she can conveniently be received. [I] have consulted with Miss Stewart on the subject. She assents to Mr. Oliver's proposal & his family arrangements. Wrote Mr. Oliver to the purposes. I put [letter] in the Post Office.

Planted some corn.

Note: "Planted some corn" in a garden located in the yard at the south side of the parsonage. A week later Rev. Muir begins making monthly payments to Mr. McGehanny for work in the garden (entry at 27 April). The parsonage in which the Muirs reside still stands (it is now known as Flounder House). Its yard is occupied by a courtyard and the congregation's Education Building.

In 1805, this space serves the private uses of the Muir family and is enclosed by a fence. Some portion of the yard serves the household as a home garden, a common practice in the eighteenth and much of the nineteenth centuries; a portion is occupied by the cow they keep; and somewhere also is a well and a privy. The parsonage's flounder-style architecture, then fairly popular in America's urban locales, explicitly seeks to make available a large a portion of the house lot for these auxiliary household uses.

21st [April, a Sunday]
Forenoon Ps[alm] 122, 1.
Afternoon Numbers 6, 22.23.24.25.26.27. 2nd [portion of] sermon [on this passage]. "I walk with you in weakness."

22nd [April]
Sally leaves us. Pay her 2$. 2$50¢ due her, for quarters end[ing] 6th April. <u>Molly Price</u> came, at 3$ a month. P[ai]d Sally 2$ 50/100 in full.

Note: Sally and Molly Price are two of several servants employed by the Muir family during the year.

23rd [April]
Received letter from Mr. R[obert] Oliver requesting Miss [Mary] S[tewart] immediately to come on [to Baltimore] by stage.

Note: Regularly scheduled stagecoach service from Alexandria to other locales along the Eastern Seaboard has existed for two decades, but travel remains arduous and slow. A letter sent via mail service, which receives the highest priority in terms of speed and travels essentially non-stop, requires nearly a week to pass between Alexandria and New York City (Brown 1943).

25th [April]

Miss [Mary] Stewart set off [for Baltimore] at 11 a.m. [this] morning. No [other] passengers [riding with her]. Paid 1$ [for passage to] Georgetown, 10$ [for passage to] Baltimore, [plus] 1$ 25/100, __ 25/100.
   Yesterday [I] Baptized <u>five children</u> of Mr. James Wilson. 40 Ladies [and] 20 Gentlemen [attend the baptism].

Note: James Wilson (1767-1805), originally from Scotland, is a local merchant and ship owner. He had served in the Revolutionary War and signed the congregation's incorporation petition to the General Assembly of the Commonwealth of Virginia in 1786. With his wife, Elizabeth Johnson Taylor Wilson, and family, he resides at 124 South Fairfax Street. They are members of the Meeting House congregation. James will die "of fever" in July (see diary entry at 9 July). The five children being baptized are – William Bruce Wilson, Marion Wilson, Ann Campbell Wilson, Malvina Allen Wilson, and Robert Johnston Taylor Wilson.

27th [April]
Paid [Mr.] McGehanny 1$ monthly for work for garden. Promised 50/100[¢] more.
   Get from C[aptain John] Tucker [a] quart [of] Salt. P[ai]d [for it]. Letters from Bermuda by C[aptain] Bell dated 11th April.
   Capt. Wm. W. Newbold sent an order for 16$ [for] Miss [Mary] Stewart's passage from Bermuda to Norfolk [and] 12$ for Mary [Muir also].

28th [April, a Sunday]
   Forenoon   Matthew 11, 28.29.30.
   Afternoon   2 Timothy 4, 6.7.8.

29[th] [April]
Paid Capt. John Tucker on Capt. [William W.] Newbold['s] order 20$, [and] afterward 8$ in full. Mr. [Andrew] Jamieson promised to put flour [and] half [barrel of his Jamieson Bakery] crackers on board the *Eve* for Capt. [Samuel] Welman [Rev. Muir's father in law] of Bermuda on my ac[coun]t.
   Hear from Mr. McLaughton that Miss [Mary] Stewart spent the afternoon of the 25[th] at his house, [and was] se[n]t off next morn[in]g in the care of Mr. Waggoner for Baltimore.

30th [April]
Wrote Capt. Welman, Mrs. Welman, Betsy & the children also. Will send the letters by Sam[ue]l on board the *Eve*.

Note: Captain Samuel and Margaret Harvey Welman are the parents of Elizabeth Welman Muir, Rev. Muir's wife. They reside in Bermuda.

5th [May, a Sunday]
  Forenoon   James 5, 11. Funeral [service for] Mrs. [Henrietta Turberville] Maffitt [late wife of Rev. William Maffitt].
  Afternoon   Luke 24, 50-end.

7th [May]
Sam[ue]l [Rev. Muir's son] and 6 boys went on Gadsby's stage to Chantilly.
  Letter [received] from [Rev.] Mr. [David] Wiley.
  [I am] still uncertain whether [I] will go to Philadelphia [to attend the General Assembly of Presbyterian Church].
  Wrote him as I have declined going. Payed Mr. Norburgh five Dollars. Payed Robert Welman at N[ew] York.
  Attend [meeting of Church] Committee.
  Wrote Robt. Lenox, Esq., N[ew] York, concerning taking my $ to Robt. Welman.
  [Rev.] Dr. [Ashbel] Green, [of] Philadelphia was appointed Delegate to the [General] Association of [Congregational Churches in] Connecticut [for 1806]. [Wrote Rev.] Mr. [John] Glendy, Baltimore, on same subject, and [Rev.] Mr. [James] Inglis.

Notes: Chantilly is the estate of Rev. William Maffitt, where he conducts the school that is attended by Samuel Muir and several other boys from Alexandria.

Rev. Muir decides not to attend the annual sessions of the General Assembly of the Presbyterian Church in the U.S.A., which convenes at Philadelphia in May. Andrew Jamieson, an elder at the Meeting House, will attend these sessions as a delegate of the Presbytery of Baltimore. Rev. Muir will instead attend the annual meeting of the General Association of Congregational Churches in Connecticut as a representative of the Presbyterian Church in June.

Robert Lenox (1759-1839), originally from Scotland, is a New York City merchant prince, who becomes one of the wealthiest merchant-businessmen in New York City prior to the emergence of the Gilded Age financiers. He is an elder of the Wall Street Presbyterian Church (later First Presbyterian Church at New York City); active in New York's St. Andrew's Society; and will become a director of the Presbyterian Church's Princeton Theological Seminary when it is created in 1812. Rev. Muir may have known Lenox from the time (1788-89) when he had filled a temporary ministerial position at the Wall Street Church. Muir and Lenox attend several General Assemblies of the Presbyterian Church in the U.S.A., Lenox as an elder commissioner from the Presbytery of New York, and Rev. Muir as a commissioner from the Presbytery of Baltimore.

Rev. Dr. Ashbel Green (1762-1848) serves Second Presbyterian Church at Philadelphia from 1787 to 1812; as stated clerk of the General Assembly of the Presbyterian Church in the U.S.A. from 1790 to 1803; as Chaplain of the U.S. Congress from 1792 to 1800; and as President of the College of New Jersey (Princeton University) from 1812 to 1822. He serves as chair of the Presbyterian Church's Standing Committee on Missions, the first sustained national mission effort of American Presbyterians, at its creation in 1802. In this position, he establishes and edits General Assembly's Missionary Magazine; or, Evangelical Intelligencer, *to which Rev. Muir contributes during 1805, its inaugural year of publication.*

8th [May]

Conveyed the Letters to Mr. [Andrew] Jamieson & Presbytery [*Minutes*] book [for him] to carry to [meeting of] Synod [of Philadelphia and General Assembly of Presbyterian Church, which will be convening in Philadelphia].

Paid Mr. [Andrew] Jamieson [for] Flour 16$50 and for Jamieson Bakery] Crackers 3$72 [which were] put on board the *Eve* for Bermuda. Paid [Dr. Elisha Cullen] Dick [for] shoes [for] Samuel [Rev. Muir's son] 2$50. Mary [one of Rev. Muir's daughters] 1$. Got sugar for Mr. __ 12$. Paid for some Brandy 2$75/100. Have paid Robert by Mr. Norburgh 5$ in full.

Note: Andrew Jamieson, an elder in the Meeting House congregation, is conveying the Minutes *book of the Presbytery of Baltimore to a Synod of Philadelphia meeting, prior to his attending the General Assembly of the Presbyterian Church in the U.S.A. at Philadelphia.*

Rev. Muir makes no record in his diary, but he performs a marriage service for John Fair Brothers and Elizabeth Ends on the 10th of May (Brumbaugh 1918-20).

11ᵗʰ [May]
Dine with Mr. William Yeaton at Gadsby's [Tavern]. Sixty six sat down at dinner. __ for different 11$^{(shilling)}$/ paid in full.

[Paid] 4$ for bonnet for Jane [Muir, Rev. Muir's oldest daughter, then seventeen].

Note: William Yeaton (1766-1834), originally from New Hampshire, is a local merchant who resides at 607 Cameron Street (known today as the Lord Fairfax House). He and his recently deceased wife, Sally Yeaton (1771-1803), are members of the Meeting House congregation.

12ᵗʰ [May, a Sunday]
Forenoon Luke 18, 9-14. 1ˢᵗ sermon [on this passage].

Afternoon Song [of Solomon] 2, 3.

Extremely wet [with rain] between Sermons.

13ᵗʰ [May]
A Letter from [Rev.] Mr. [David] Wiley enclosing conference [report of meetings of General] Assembly. His let[ter] __ go 25[indecipherable monetary denomination]25/100. Answered [Rev.] Mr. Wiley's letter, sending [it] to him by Mr. [Andrew] Jamieson. Post it on 14ᵗʰ in [post] office.

Payd Newton [and] Ricketts for flour 1½ barrels, 16$ [on] 15ᵗʰ, __ 2 lbs. butter – ¼ doz. eggs 2 __, __ . Jacob's __ 13sh[illings]/6. Stevenson work in full 10sh[illings]/6.

Note: William Newton (1765-1814) and John Thomas Ricketts (1754-1821) are partners in ownership of a flour mill on Cameron Run west of Alexandria, and a store in town at the southeast corner of Fairfax and Prince streets. William Newton and his wife, Jane Barr Stuart Newton (1776-1815), are both members of the Meeting House congregation. John Ricketts and his wife, Mary Barr Ricketts (1754-1820), reside on Prince Street, and are also members of the congregation.

17ᵗʰ [May]

Give [to General Assembly of the Presbyterian Church for support of] mission 5$.

A [Rev.] Mr. [Thomas] Robbins, Clergyman from Massachusetts [is] in Town. Breakfast with [him] on 18th. [indecipherable payments].

1$ [to] Mary [Muir, Rev. Muir's second daughter, for a] bonnet.

A letter [received] from Sam[ue]l [Rev. Muir's son] which I answered. Send him stockings __ .

Note: Rev. Dr. Thomas Robbins (1777-1856) is a Congregational minister from Norfolk, Connecticut who stops to visit with Rev. Muir and perhaps a relative while returning to New England from Ohio. He had been serving as a missionary in Ohio, sponsored by the General Association of Massachusetts in conjunction with the Plan of Union between Congregationalists and Presbyterians (General Association 1805, Robbins 1886-87). He will preach on Sunday afternoon. Isaac Robbins (1779-1846), who is perhaps a relative of the Rev. Robbins – he is also from Massachusetts – operates a dry goods business on King Street.

18th [May]

Payed General [Assembly of Presbyterian Church] 10$ in full.

Note: The $10 sent to the General Assembly is in support of the Presbyterian Church's initial denominational missionary effort – the Standing Committee on Missions – which provides assistance such as disaster relief to people in need, and the support of missionary efforts to American Indians and to European Americans on the western settlement frontier.

19th [May, a Sunday]

Forenoon   Luke 18, 9-14. 2nd sermon [on this passage].
Afternoon [Rev.] Mr. [Thomas] Robbins Preached. Malachi 3, 8–.

Notes: Rev. Muir's responds positively to the Rev. Robbins – "He is a good preacher, and appears to be a well-informed and pious young man" – and provides him with a letter of introduction to the Rev. Dr. Ashbel Green at Philadelphia, whom he will visit (Letter from Muir to Green 21 May 1805).

20th [May]

Dine at Mr. [Jonathan] Swift's [residence]. Baptize his child [Mary Selina Swift].

Mr. P__ Virginia came with two daughters to spend day [and] night with us. Got leg of mutton from Gadsby's [Tavern]. The Ladies drank tea at Mr. [John] Dundas'. Mr. __ and Mrs. __ at Mr. T[homas] Vowell's. Baptize his child [Robert Harper Vowell].

A letter from Mr. [Andrew] Jamieson, mak[in]g known my appointment [and that I will travel] to Connecticut [to] attend the [annual meeting of the] General Association [of Congregational Churches taking place] there [beginning] on 23rd [of June].

Notes: "Got leg of mutton from Gadsby's Tavern" – imagine, carryout food service in 1805! Gadsby's Tavern is one of Alexandria's major inns. It is located on Royal Street, four blocks north of the parsonage. With relatively good road access to its agriculturally rich Virginia hinterland and excellent water access to the broad array of goods produced in the Chesapeake and Atlantic realms, Rev. Muir's Alexandria provides a remarkably modern array of food and drink opportunities, including a leg of lamb as a carry-out item (Sorin 1981 and 1982, Mackay 2000, Robinson 2007-08, Voges 1977).

John Dundas (1759-1813) is an Alexandria merchant, former member of the Common Council and former Mayor, and treasurer of the Meeting House congregation's Church Committee. He and his wife, Agnes Hepburn Dundas (1770-1820), reside on the south side of Pendleton Street, between Washington and Columbus. Rev. Muir's memorial sermon at the death of John Dundas is published as The Mortal and Immortal State, a Sermon; This Sermon, Delivered at Alexandria, on the 5th of September, in Testimony of Great Respect for the Memory of John Dundas, Esq., a Native of Philadelphia: Who Died on the 30th of August 1813, in the 55th Year of His Age, is Offered to Surviving Friends with Sympathy from the Author *(Muir 1813).*

Robert Harper Vowell, the son of Thomas and Mary Harper Vowell, members of the Meeting House congregation, will survive only until September. His mother will pass away on the 13th of August 1805 (see entry).

The General Association of Congregational Churches in Connecticut had joined with the General Assembly of the Presbyterian Church in a "Plan of Union" in 1801 to work co-operatively in establishing new congregations in western New York State and Ohio, areas then opening to settlement by Americans of European origin. The joint venture between the two denominations, who are later joined by the Congregational Associations of Massachusetts, Vermont, and New Hampshire, continues until 1852. In a month, Rev. Muir will lead the delegation from the Presbyterian Church to the annual meeting of the General Association at Guilford, Connecticut. This is the second annual meeting of the General Association to be attended by Rev. Muir – in 1799, he represented the Presbyterian Church at the Association's meeting at Hartford, Connecticut along with Rev. Dr. John Rodgers of New York City and Rev. Dr. Robert Finley of Basking Ridge, New Jersey (Sweet 1936, Noricks 1982, Gaustad and Noll 2003).

On 24th went on to Baltimore. On 22[nd] Betsy [family name is indecipherable] hired at 3$ a month.

Note: Betsy is one of several female servants employed by the Muir family during the year.

25th [May]
Wrote Sam[ue]l [Rev. Muir's son]. [Rev.] Mr. [William] Maffitt promised him a __ provided a horse can be procured.

26th [May, a Sunday]
Forenoon 1 Cor[inthians] 1, 30.
Afternoon Jo[hn] 3, 7. 1st sermon [on this passage]

Note: Rev. Muir will preach on this text from John, "Do not be astonished that I said to you, 'You must be born from above'," on his upcoming trip at Baltimore, New York City, and Stratford and Middletown, Connecticut.

27th [May]
Go to Chantilly [to visit Rev.] Mr. [William] Maffitt [who is] in bad health. Have a Note from Mr. [James] Irvin.

Note: James Irvin, also "James Irwin" (1757-1822), is originally from Belfast, Ireland. He operates a rope-making business on the Alexandria waterfront; serves as a justice of the peace; was a charter member of the Alexandria Library Company; signed both the famous Memorial and Remonstrance *to disestablish the Episcopal Church in Virginia in 1785 and the Meeting House congregation's incorporation petition in 1786; and is a member of St.*

Andrew's Society. He is an elder in the Presbyterian Church and a member of the Meeting House's Church Committee. He attends several meetings of the Presbytery of Baltimore and of the General Assembly of the Presbyterian Church as a commissioner from the Presbytery of Baltimore.

28th [May]
Return to Newton's Mills.

Note: Newton's Mill, also known as Lane's Mill, includes both grist and saw mills. It is located near Chantilly, the estate of Rev. Maffitt, and Sully, the estate of Richard Bland Lee, in the vicinity of present-day Centerville, Virginia.

29th [May]
Get [back] to town. [Conduct] society [i.e., the group of members who convene for midweek prayer-worship] in the evening.

Wrote [Rev.] Mr. W[illiam] Williamson [for] Supply here last Lord's day [of] June, [Rev.] Mr. [William] Hill first [of] July, [Rev.] Mr. __, third Lord's day [of] July. Put [Rev.] Mr. Hill's and [Rev.] __'s letters in the Post Office. Mr. __ took charge of the letter to [Rev.] Mr. [William] Williamson.

Note: Rev. Dr. William Hill (1769-1852) serves the Presbyterian Church at Winchester, Virginia from 1800 to 1834. Described by one church historian as a "controversialist," he becomes deeply involved in promoting the Old School-New School division of the Presbyterian Church in the 1830s. He serves as minister of the Second Presbyterian Church at Alexandria from 1836 to 1838 (Dow 1952).

2nd [June, a Sunday]
Forenoon   John 13, 34.35.
Afternoon   John 3, 7. 2nd sermon [on this passage].
A pair of boots for [Dr. Elisha Cullen] Dick 5$ 25/100. P[ai]d 5$25/100.

Note: Rev. Muir makes no entry here, but he performs a marriage service for John Harper and Sarah Davis on the 5th of June. (Brumbaugh 1918-20).

6th [June]

Set off at 8 in morning; arriving at 10 at Georgetown [in the District of Columbia]. Met stage to Baltimore. Arrived at 9 a.m. o'clock on 7th [having traveled overnight from Georgetown].

At 12 [noon], go to Philadelphia where I am at 11 [a.m.] on 8th [having traveled overnight from Baltimore].

Note: Rev. Muir is heading north on a journey that will take him to Baltimore, Philadelphia, New York City, and eventually to Connecticut to attend the annual meetings of the General Association of Congregational Churches in Connecticut. He will be away for a month, not returning to Alexandria until the eighth of July.

9th [June, a Sunday at] Arch Street [Presbyterian Church, which is formally known as Second Presbyterian Church. It is located at Arch and Third streets in Philadelphia]
[Rev.] Dr. Mc__ morning.
Afternoon John 13, 34.35.

Note: The Rev. Dr. Mc__ remains unidentified. The senior minister at Second Presbyterian is the Rev. Dr. Ashbel Green, who also serves as editor of General Assembly's Missionary Magazine. *Rev. Muir corresponds with the Rev. Green during the year when he contributes a series of articles titled "Nebuchadnezzar." Rev. Green's associate is the Rev. Dr. Jacob J. Janeway, who attends meetings of the General Association of Congregational Churches of Connecticut with Rev. Muir in a week's time. Rev. Dr. Mc__ preaches at the morning service; Rev. Muir in the afternoon.*

10th [June]
On the stage for New York [City]. Arrive at 7 of [the] 11th [after traveling overnight from Philadelphia]. [Stay with] Mr. [Robert] Lenox. Dine at Mr. Lenox's. Call at [Rev.] Dr. [John] Rodgers, __ , and [Dr. James] Tillary.

Notes: Robert Lenox's town house is at 53 Fifth Avenue, near 12th Street, a few blocks south of what will become Union Square.

Rev. Dr. John Rodgers (1727-1811) serves both the Wall Street (later First) Presbyterian Church and the Brick Presbyterian Church at New York City from 1788 to 1809. The Wall Street Church, dating from 1719, is located on Wall Street between Broadway and Nassau streets; the Brick Church, which dates from 1766, is on Beekman Street between Park Row and Nassau streets. Rev. Rodgers served as moderator of the first General Assembly of the Presbyterian Church in the U.S.A., which was convened in Philadelphia in 1789. In that same year, the Revs. Muir and Jedidiah Morse both had sought to serve as a collegiate pastor with Rev. Rodgers, but both ended up taking other calls.

Dr. James Tillary, also "James Tillery" (1756-1818), is a native of Scotland who trained as a medical doctor at the University of Edinburgh. He practices medicine in New York City for over forty years at his office at the corner of Wall Street and Broadway, and serves as President of New York's St. Andrew's Society. Rev. Muir was an honorary member of New York's St. Andrew's Society and also served for many years as chaplain of the St. Andrew's Society at Alexandria.

12th [June]

Dine at L[ieutenan]t Governor [John] Broome's.

Notes: John Broome (1738-1810) is a New York City merchant who serves as the Lieutenant Governor of the State of New York from 1804 until his death in 1810. He too is a member of Wall Street (First) Presbyterian Church.

A 1,500-word essay arguing against the practice of dueling by the Rev. Timothy Dwight IV, President of Yale College, appears in the Alexandria newspaper this day. Dwight's expository argument begins – "Go with me to yonder church-yard. Whose is the newly opened Grave? Yester-day he was himself, a creature of hope, a probationer for immortality...Where is he now? His soul has ascended to God, with all its sins upon his head, to be judged and condemned to wretchedness, which has no end... " (Alexandria Daily Advertiser *12 June 1805 p. 3).*

13th [June]

Dine at Mr. __. Rode with Mr. __. Had breakfast with him. Met Miss Johnston at tea at his house.

[Take] the stage with Robert [space left blank by Rev. Muir]. [Arrive at] Stratford.

Notes: Stratford is a coastal Connecticut town between New York City and New Haven.

While Rev. Muir is away from Alexandria, a new map of the Commonwealth of Virginia is being promoted for a week back home at Gadsby's Tavern. The large-size map is designed for *public display on walls, and will become famous as the "Bishop Madison Map of Virginia" when it is issued in 1807 – it measures 34¼ by 53 inches. Notices announcing the availability of preliminary materials for examination, and the opportunity to support the map's publication through subscription, appear in the* Alexandria Daily Advertiser *from the 13th to the 21st of June.*

15th [June]
At [space for Christian name left blank by Rev. Muir] Walhert Esq. ___.
Meet [Rev.] Mr. [Nash] Legrand on stage. Stopped at Dr. ___ from Dr. Lewis. At Stratford.

Note: Rev. Nash Legrand (1768-1814) is a Presbyterian minister who serves several congregations in the Presbytery of Winchester in the Shenandoah Valley. Rev. Nash, along with Rev. Muir and Rev. Jacob J. Janeway, form the delegation of the Presbyterian Church to the annual meeting of the General Association of Congregational Churches in Connecticut that is about to convene.

16th [June, a Sunday] At Stratford.
Forenoon   S[ong of Solomon] 2, 3.
Afternoon   Jo[hn] 3, 7.

Note: Rev. Muir delivers these sermons at Stratford, Connecticut.

17th [June]
Go to New Haven [Connecticut] with Robt. [space left blank by Rev. Muir]. Set off about 10 [a.m]. Get there by 2 [p.m.], about 20 miles.

[New Haven is a] beautiful town. The College [Yale] delightfully situated [with] 200 students. See [Rev.] Mr. [Jeremiah] Day. Dine at Inn. Tea [with] Hezekiah Frith Sr. from Bermuda. His son [is a] promising youth. [Rev.] Mr. [Nash] Legrand and [Rev.] Mr. [Jacob J.] Janeway arrive in the evening.

Notes: Rev. Muir returns to visit the college that had awarded him an honorary Doctor of Divinity (D.D.) degree in 1791.

Rev. Dr. Jeremiah Day (1773-1867) is a Congregational minister and professor of mathematics and natural philosophy in Yale College at the time of Rev. Muir's visit. He spent 1801-02 in Bermuda, and will serve as President of Yale College from 1817 to 1847.

Rev. Muir takes tea with Hezekiah Frith, Senior (1763-1848), of Warwick, Bermuda, where he had served as minister of Christ Church (Church of Scotland) from 1781 to 1788. Frith is a wealthy ship owner, whose three daughters all marry Presbyterian ministers. Hezekiah, Junior (1786-1851), the "promising youth," will soon enter the clergy (Kennedy 1964).

Rev. Dr. Jacob J. Janeway (1774-1858) serves as a minister at Philadelphia's Second Presbyterian Church and as stated clerk of the General Assembly of the Presbyterian Church.

Revs. Muir, Legrand, and Janeway form the delegation from the Presbyterian Church to the annual meeting of the General Association of Congregational Churches in Connecticut

18th [June]

Set off for Gilford [Guilford], 17 miles [further along the coast from New Haven].

[Attend t]he [General] Association [of Congregational Churches in Connecticut] meet[ing]. Lodge at Mr. Griffins. Mr. Brown there. No servants. All conducted with care. The house neat. Everything in order.

[Rev.] Mr. [John] Foot[e], [serves as] moderator [of General Association meeting]. [Rev] Messrs Chapin [and] Goodrich, scribes. [Rev. Dr. Jacob] Janeway preached in the e[ven]ing.

Notes: Guilford is a coastal town east of New Haven, Connecticut. The meetings of the General Association are conducted in the home of the Rev. Israel Brainerd (1772-1854), who serves the Congregational Church at Guilford.

Rev. John Foote (1742-1813) is a Congregational minister serving the Congregational Church at Cheshire, Connecticut.

Rev. Calvin Chapin is a Congregational minister serving the Congregational Church at Wethersfield, Connecticut. He serves as scribe for the General Association meeting.

Rev. Samuel Goodrich (1763-1835), a Congregational minister who serves the First Congregational Church at Ridgefield, Connecticut from 1786 to 1811, is serving at these meetings of the General Association as assistant scribe. He will represent the General Association of Connecticut at the General Assembly of the Presbyterian Church in 1806. He is the father of Charles Augustus Goodrich (1790-1862), a Congregational minister and writer, and the writer Samuel Griswold Goodrich (1793-1860), whose histories, geographies, and biographies for youth, using the pen name of Peter Parley, sell more than seven million copies prior to the Civil War.

19th [June]

At [the meeting of the General] Association, I preached.

[Rev.] Mr. [Nash] Legrand to go [ahead of me] with [Rev. Calvin] Chapin to Middleto[w]n [Connecticut]. Dine at [Rev.] Mr. [Samuel] Goodrich's. [Arrive] at Middleto[w]n [at] 5 o'clock – 20 miles [inland]. Mrs. Williams infirm, well situated.

Notes: "I preached" refers to Rev. Muir's preaching on the afternoon of that day's sessions. Minutes of the session note – "At three o'clock, p.m. [all] attended public worship, when a sermon was preached by Dr. Muir, from John xiii.34,35. And a second sermon by Mr. LeGrand, from the 1st epistle of John 1 and a part of the 3d verse." (General Association of Connecticut 1805 p. 7).

The General Association's Minutes indicate that Rev. Muir serves with the Revs. Backus, Parsons, and Ely on the annual meeting's Committee on Overtures, and that the following statement concerning revival activities in the Presbyterian Church is read at the meeting – "The Report of the delegate of the last General Assembly of the Presbyterian Church was read. It stated that very extraordinary accounts were presented to the Assembly, relative to bodily exercises attending religious services in Kentucky, Tennessee, and some other sections of the Southern States." (General Association of Connecticut 1805 p. 6; a detailed account of the actions taken by the General Assembly of 1805 are in Presbyterian Church in the U.S.A. 1847*).*

Intense religious revivals known as camp meetings, some of which involve crowds numbering in the thousands, had occurred for several years, first in the trans-Appalachian area centered on the Cumberland River, and then spreading eastward as far as New England. Among the leaders of the earliest large western revivals are several Presbyterians ministers, including the Rev. James McGready and Rev. Barton W. Stone among others in the Presbytery of Cumberland, Synod of Kentucky. Come 1810, the Presbytery of Cumberland will break with the Presbyterian Church in the U.S.A. and form the Cumberland Presbyterian Church as a separate denomination. Issues associated with religious revivals, church doctrine, and beliefs that are raised by these groups, and with the very nature of Protestant religious denominations, loom large on public agendas up and down the Eastern

*Seaboard at this time as well. One Alexandria book store advertises the availability of a 250-page tract presenting a point-by-point argument against established Presbyterian practices prepared by clergy from the Cumberland River Valley for half the year (*Alexandria Daily Advertiser *May through late December 1805). The work is,* An Abstract of an Apology, for Removing the Jurisdiction of the Synod of Kentucky, Being a Compendious View of the Gospel, and a Few Remarks on the Confession of Faith, *by Robert Marshall, John Dunlavy, Richard McNemar, Barton W. Stone, and John Thompson (Lexington, Kentucky: Joseph Charless, 1804). (Commentary on these revivals is provided by Boles 1972, Bruce 1974, Cross 1950, and Glazier 2005.)*

Middletown, Connecticut is located twenty miles north (inland) of Guilford, on the Connecticut River.

The "Mrs. Williams" that Rev. Muir visits is Martha Cornell Williams, an in-law, and the wife of Capt. Benjamin Williams from Bermuda (Letter from Muir to Green, 7 May 1805).

23rd [June, a Sunday]
Forenoon   Jo[hn] 3, 7.
Afternoon   Jo[hn] 13, 34-35.
At Middleto[w]n.

Note: Rev. Muir delivers these sermons at Middletown, Connecticut. The specific reason for traveling to Middletown to preach is not known. Perhaps he is retracing the footsteps of the great eighteenth-century English evangelist George Whitefield (1714-1770), who was familiar to Rev. Muir from his having served at the church in Bermuda where Whitefield had also preached.

Whitefield had preached to a crowd of worshippers at Middletown estimated to have been four thousand in number.

24th [June]
Return to New Haven. Get on board a Packet. Found Mr. [Russell] Goodrich there, who once lived at Alex[andri]a. On water [between New Haven and New York City through the night of] 25th.

[Arrive] at New York [City on] 26th. Dine with [Rev.] Dr. [John] Rodgers, Mr. [Robert] Lenox, his children Elizabeth, Alethea, Isabella, Rachel, Charlotte, Jennet, James, Mary [and] Henrietta.

Notes: *Russell Goodrich, a graduate of Yale College, is known to Rev. Muir from the period when he taught at the Alexandria Academy (1786 into the 1790s), and from his involvement with the Alexandria Society for the Promotion of Useful Knowledge, which Muir had worked to establish (Crothers 2001).*

Rev. Muir writes about the "religious impressions" experienced by the Lenox children in his pamphlet, The Young Christian: An Instructive Narrative *(1807). James Lenox (1800-1880), now just five years of age, will follow in his father's footsteps and become a trustee of Princeton Theological Seminary, to which he will donate land, the Lenox House (still in use), and a library in 1845.*

27th [June]
Dine __ .

28th [June]
[At] Mr. Mitchell's [in New York City].

Note: Rev. Muir had visited with Mr. Mitchell when he stopped in New York City on his way to Connecticut.

29th [June]
[At] Dr. __ . Spent one night at Mr. __'s country house. Rode out with Mr. [Robert] Lenox to his country house.

Note: The Lenox family's country house is located at the Lenox Farm, a property that will come to be incorporated into New York City and its grid of streets between Fourth and Fifth Avenues from 68th to 74th streets. When the farm comes to be divided into lots, it forms the Lenox Hill neighborhood and provides homes for the Union Theological Seminary, Presbyterian Hospital, and Lenox Library, all of which are funded by James Lenox, Robert Lenox's only son. Each of these institutions subsequently relocates. The Lenox Library is replaced by the residence of Henry C. Frick (home of The Frick Collection today), when the library's collection is incorporated into the New York Public Library.

30th [June, a Sunday]
  Forenoon Acts 11, 26.
  Afternoon Jo[hn] 13, 34-35.
  Evening Jo[hn] 3, 7.

At New York [City].

Dine at [Rev.] Dr. [John] McKnight's and drink tea there. Then evening with Dr. [James] Tillary.

Notes: Notes: Rev. Muir delivers sermons this day at the Wall Street Presbyterian Church.
Rev. Dr. John McKnight (1754-1823) is collegiate minister with Rev. Dr. John Rodgers at Wall Street Presbyterian and Brick Presbyterian congregations, from 1789 to 1809. He had served as moderator of the General Assembly of the Presbyterian Church in the U.S.A. in 1791, and subsequently serves as President of Dickinson College in Carlisle, Pennsylvania. Rev. Muir had prepared a pastoral letter with him at the General Assembly of the Presbyterian Church in 1799 that was to be read to congregations.

2nd [July] Dine at Mr. Lenox's with [Rev.] Dr. [John] Rodgers, Mason, [Rev. Samuel] Miller, [Dr. James] Tillary, and __ Mitchell.

Note: Rev. Dr. Samuel Miller (1769-1850) is the minister of two Presbyterian congregations in New York City and subsequently joins the faculty of Princeton Theological Seminary, where he serves from 1813 to 1850. Miller Chapel at Princeton Theological Seminary is named for him.

3rd [July]
Go to Princeton [New Jersey]. At [Rev.] Dr. [Samuel] Smith's all night. Mr. M__ Polard __.
Get to Philadelphia on the 3rd [actually the 4th]. There on the 4th [5th] Dine at Mr. Lile's. Go on the ev[ening] stage. Get to Baltimore on the 6th.

Notes: Rev. Dr. Samuel Stanhope Smith (1751-1819) is a Presbyterian minister, who serves as President of the College of New Jersey (Princeton University) from 1795 to 1812. He had earlier been the founding President of Hampden-Sydney College in Virginia.

While Rev. Muir is in Philadelphia during the celebration of Independence Day, Edmund Jennings Lee delivers the Washington Society's biannual fundraising lecture in Alexandria for the

Academy that Rev. Muir oversees. (*Alexandria Daily Advertiser* 9 July 1805 p. 2).

7th [July, a Sunday]
Forenoon   Jo[hn] 13, 34-35.
Afternoon Jo[hn] 3, 7.

Note: These two sermons are delivered in the First Presbyterian Church at Baltimore.

Get to Alexandria on [Monday] the 8th.
On 9th visit Mr. James Wilson whom I found dying. He died in the evening. Attended [presided at] funeral on the 10th. Made a number of calls.
Prepare for Public Service [Sunday worship services] on 9th 11th 12th 13th.
Several y[oun]g men killed by lightening at mill near Dumfries. Among others a Mr. Janney, his mother a widow; [he was someone] to whom she looked up [esteemed].

Notes: Rev. Muir does not here make note of local weather conditions, but temperatures are in the mid-to-high 90s throughout this week (Miller 1992).

*James Wilson (1767-1805) is a member of the congregation. His family's five children were baptized by Rev. Muir less than three months earlier (entry at 25 April). Rev. Muir presides at his memorial service, announced by two articles in that morning's newspaper, "Yesterday evening departed this life Mr. James Wilson, Merchant, aged 38 years. His friends and acquaintances are invited to attend his funeral from his own home, this evening at half past five o'clock" and "Brethren of Lodge No. 22 will please meet at their Lodge-Room, this evening, at half past five o'clock, for the purpose of attending the funeral of deceased Brother James Wilson; by order of the Master, D. Murgatroyd, Sec'y" (*Alexandria Daily Advertiser *Wednesday 10 July 1805). He is interred in the Burial Ground of the Meeting House.*

Dumfries, Virginia is in Prince William County, south of Alexandria. Several Janney families are members of the Meeting House congregation. Rev. Muir had married Moses Janney and Judith Lawrence in February.

14th [July, a Sunday]
Forenoon   Isaiah 38, 1.

Afternoon Song [of Solomon] 2, 3.

15th [July]
Mr. Donaldson [and] Miss [Anne Donaldson] Fairfax [visit] here. Mr. [John] Dundas sick. The Boys at Chantilly [Rev. William Maffitt's estate and school] have been sick but are better.

Payd Wm. Ramsay 40$ for [Rev.] Mr. Maffitt, and gave him a check for 48$, eight [dollars] I received from him. Sent 7 [dollars] by Dawson, one [dollar] due to [Rev.]Mr. Maffitt – the sum due [Rev.] Mr. Maffitt first of July last.

Notes: Anne Donaldson Fairfax is the daughter of Bryan (Lord) Fairfax (1736-1802) and his second wife, Jane Donaldson Fairfax, also as "Jennie Dennison" Fairfax (unknown-1805). Jane Donaldson Fairfax passed away two weeks earlier, on the 1st of July, at Mount Eagle, the family estate in Fairfax County just south of Hunting Creek. Mr. Donaldson is a relative.

William Ramsay (1787-1822), son of Colonel Dennis Ramsay (1754-1810), is a merchant whose business is located on King St. He is a member of the Meeting House congregation.

18th [July]
__ for Hartshorne cook 33 [shillings]/.

19th Walk to Mr. [James] Irvin's. Dine there and return.

Note: Rev. Muir probably walks to James Irvin's country estate, which is located on the south side of Cameron Run about a mile west of Alexandria.

21st [July, a Sunday]
Forenoon Isaiah 28, 16. Call clause ["One who trusts will not panic."] First sermon [on this passage].
Afternoon Mark 4, 11–.

On 22nd [receive] letter from Bermuda by the way of New York. Capt. [Samuel] Welman has been extremely ill since Jane's death & __ both since & before. [They] had received flour [and] crackers sent by the *Eve* [on the] 29th April last.

Notes: Captain Samuel Welman of Bermuda is the father of Elizabeth Muir, Rev. Muir's wife.

Virginia Edmund Jennings Randolph (1753-1813) places a notice of considerable length in the local Alexandria newspaper requesting contributions to his proposed Statistical View of Virginia *on the 22nd. The proposed work is a geographical-historical account of the Commonwealth of Virginia, common during this early national period, for which Randolph is seeking local expertise. The never-completed manuscript is issued in fragmentary form a century and a half later (*Alexandria Daily Advertiser *22 July 1805 p. 2, Randolph 1970). The contributions Randolph may have received from Alexandria remain unknown.*

23rd [July]

A letter from Col. Capt. Lewis Nicholas [from] Washington [D.C.] in order to join in Com[mittee] with Mr. [William] Lowry. Prepared a certificate in favor on 24th which I signed and left with Mr. [Andrew] Jamieson to sign and forward. During my visit at Connecticut, a letter arrived at Alex[andri]a from [Rev.] Dr. [Jedidiah] Morse informing me that I had been chosen a member of the Massachusetts Society for Promoting The Knowledge [and] soliciting my aid to the *Panoplist*, a monthly religious publication. Answered his letter on 25th. [I] promised aid with my Pen to the *Panoplist*, and begged my thanks to be given the Massachusetts Society for the honor conferred upon me.

Notes: Rev. Muir utilizes the ranks of both Colonel and Captain when referring to Lewis Nicholas. The practice of referring to Nicholas by a variety of ranks appears common. Nicholas serves on a committee of Alexandria's Washington Society (more information on him is presented in an entry note for the 22nd of February).

William Lowry is an Alexandria merchant who had signed the petition to incorporate the Alexandria Academy. He is a member of the Meeting House congregation and serves as a member of the congregation's Church Committee.

Rev. Dr. Jedidiah Morse (1761-1826) is a Congregational minister serving the First Congregational Church at Charlestown, Massachusetts. He had visited the Meeting House in 1785 and visited George Washington at Mount Vernon with the Rev. Dr. Isaac Stockton Keith, who then served the Meeting House congregation (information on Rev. Keith is at the diary entry for the 28th of November). Revs. Morse and Muir have known each other for at least twenty years (see notes for the 10th of June). Morse is a member of the Board of Overseers at Harvard College, was a founder of Andover Theological Seminary, and the author of America's first published works in geography, including Geography Made Easy *(1784),* American Geography *(1789), and* American Universal Geography *(1793). Rev. Muir contributes to the* Panoplist, *the new periodical established by Morse, during the year.*

"Massachusetts Society for Promoting The Knowledge" is the Massachusetts Society for Promoting Christian Knowledge, established in 1803. It is the first organization in America devoted solely to the publication of religious works (Nord 2002).

Rev. Muir makes no record in his diary, but he performs a marriage service for William C. R. Smith and Mary Morgan during the week (Brumbaugh 1918-20).

28th [July, a Sunday]
Forenoon Is[aiah] 28, 16. 2nd sermon [on this passage].
Afternoon Luke 19, 8.9.10.

31st [July]
T[ravel to] Mr. [Walter D.] Addison, attending the examination of [the students in] his school. The boys requited themselves well.

Yesterday Mr. [John] Peter, one [of the] clerks of Bank of Columbia, on the road from Georgetown [to Alexandria], with 17,000$ to be exchanged in the Bank of Alex[andri]a was attacked 2 miles from Alex[andri]a by a genteel looking man, who rushing from the bushes, secured the bridle of his horse, fired a pistol without speaking. The contents [of the pistol] entered his body, [and he was] knocked senseless upon the ground. [He] was left to [the assistance of] Mr. [Jonathan] Swift. __ found the money involved was taken __ . This happened at 12 a.m. on a frequented road, where passengers are going every instant. The wound not likely to be fatal. An inhabitant [of Alexandria], name of [John Atkins] Burford, [has been] taken [into custody], suspicions [are] that he is perpetrator.

Notes: Walter D. Addison conducts a school at Oxon Hill, his 500-acre estate in Prince Georges County, Maryland, which is immediately across the Potomac River from Alexandria. The estate was originally owned and developed by Thomas Addison. (Oxon Hill is today operated by the Maryland-National Capital Park and Planning Commission as a living museum.)

*It is John Peter, or John Peters, clerk of the Bank of Columbia who has been shot. A reward has been offered for the arrest and conviction of his assailant. Local newspaper accounts refer to the incident as "the most daring robbery ever perpetrated in America...[and that] about 150 of the inhabitants of Alexandria were engaged in the pursuit [of the perpetrators]." The amount of money stolen totals to the considerable sum of $18,115. Rev. Muir attends the trial of the accused, John Atkins Burford, which he refers to elsewhere in his diary as a "theatre trial." It occurs in December. (*Alexandria Daily Advertiser *1 August 1805 p. 3, 3 August p. 4, and 9 August p. 3, Miller 1988 pp. 171-72).*

The residence of Jonathan Swift, Colross, is located in the 1100-block of Oronoco Street. It is one of the few large residences located on the northern outskirts of Alexandria.

John Atkins Burford is an Alexandria shopkeeper who sells fruit. He is apprehended almost immediately. However, notices offering a $1,000 reward for the recovery of the money, bank notes, and other financial instruments, and a $500 reward for the apprehension of the perpetrator appear in local newspapers for days. Burford will be charged but not convicted for this crime, and in spite of being acquitted of any wrongdoing, he is subsequently imprisoned without further charges. His appeal for release wins a unanimous decision by the U.S. Supreme Court in February 1806 (diary entries made during the trial are at 16 and 17 December).

4th [August, a Sunday]
Forenoon Ps[alm] 24, 1–.
Afternoon Heb[rews] 7, 19.

5th [August]
Having prepared notes on Nebuchadnezzar's character – "Neb[uchadnezzar] Corrupted," [I] sent it by Post [to Rev.] Dr. [Ashbel] Green [in Philadelphia] for publication in *Assembly [Missionary] Magazine.*

Note: "Nebuchadnezzar Corrupted" appears as "Nebuchadnezzar," the first of four installments of an article that Rev. Muir publishes in General Assembly's Missionary Magazine; or, Evnagellical Intelligencer. *Installments appear in August, September, November, and December.* General Assembly's Missionary Magazine *is a new publication of the General Assembly of the*

Presbyterian Church that is edited by the Rev. Dr. Ashbel Green at Philadelphia. It appears from January 1805 through December 1809.

7th [August]

Enoch Lyles __ fell [killed] by hand [of John] Bowie in [a] duel, disgraceful.

Note: Enoch Magruder Lyles of Alexandria and John F. Bowie of Piscataway, Maryland, located south of Alexandria on the Potomac River, dueled at Johnson's Spring, Virginia, also south of Alexandria. The day after the duel, the newspaper led its account of the event with "It is with regret we announce the sacrifice of a victim at the shrine of the sanguinary practice of dueling..." (Alexandria Daily Advertiser *8 August 1805 p. 3). Public notice that John Bowie had "demanded satisfaction due a* gentleman" *of Enoch Lyles had appeared in the local newspaper several weeks earlier (*Alexandria Daily Advertiser *24 July 1805 p. 3).*

*A subsequent account by the survivor, John F. Bowie, refers to the purported cause – "[I]n the course of conversation Mr. Lyles spoke of some ladies of my acquaintance in terms which I considered highly improper... " (*Alexandria Daily Advertiser *24 August 1805 p. 2). Several Lyles families are members of the Meeting House congregation. Enoch Lyles is buried in the church yard of St. John's (Episco-pal) Church at Broad Creek, Maryland, across the Potomac River just south of Alexandria.*

The practice of settling affairs of honor by means of a duel with deadly weapons continues locally until at least the 1850s. In 1825, Meeting House congregation member Captain James McGuire and fellow Alexandrian Colonel Adam Lynn engage in a duel with pistols that ends in a draw after both fire wildly inaccurate shots (McCarty 1976).

8th [August]

Received two copies of the "Panoplist." Two Numbers, 26 cent postage. Mr. Tho[mas] Vowell returned [to Alexandria].
Mrs. [Lucy Carter] Fitzhugh worse.

Notes: Thomas Vowell (1769-1845), originally from England, owns a local shipping business. He and his wife, Mary Harper Vowell (1772-1805), are members of Rev. Muir's congregation, and he serves the church as an elder. The family residence, which he constructed, is at 619 Water Street (today's South Lee Street; the residence is now known as the Snowden House).

Lucy Carter Fitzhugh passes away in a few days (diary entry for 11 August). She is the wife of William Fitzhugh and a daughter of Robert "King" Carter. William Fitzhugh (1741-1809), son of Colonel William Fitzhugh, is known as William Fitzhugh of Ravensworth, the name taken from his Fairfax County estate. Rev. Muir works closely with William Fitzhugh in conjunction with the Washington Society. The Fitzhugh family's town residence during the winter social season is at 607 Oronoco Street.

9th [August]

Andrew Watson died. Buried on 10th next [day]. He was 23 years 11 months old. [In the] address at grave [I] h[a]d my eye upon events [of the] week – [Rev. Muir is referring to the death of Enoch Lyles in a duel; several lines of indecipherable text follow] "Thou shall not kill" is com[mandment; followed by other lines of indecipherable text].

Note: Andrew Watson (1782-1805) is the son of Josiah and Mary Watson, members of the Meeting House congregation. Josiah Watson is a merchant and justice of the peace for Fairfax County. He had served as a trustee of the Alexandria Academy at its establishment in 1785; signed the famous Memorial and Remonstrance to disestablish the Episcopal Church in Virginia *in 1785; and signed the congregation's incorporation petition to the Commonwealth of Virginia in 1786. Notice of Andrew's death in the local newspaper reads, "Died last evening, Mr. Andrew Watson, of this town. His friends and acquaintances are requested to attend his funeral from the home of Mrs. Allison this evening at 5 o'clock."* (Alexandria Daily Advertiser *10 August 1805 p. 3)*

11th [August, a Sunday]

Forenoon Exodus 20, 1.2.3.4.5.6.7. [This is the first in a set of sermons he delivers on the Ten Commandments. Rev. Muir will work through all of the commandments in five sermons. At the end of the year his complete set of commentary on the commandments begins appearing as "The Decalogue" in the *Panoplist.*]

B[ein]g feverish, and my face much swollen, no service [in] the afternoon.

Mrs. [Lucy Carter] Fitzhugh wife of W[illia]m Fitzhugh Esq., died this evening.

12th [August]
Continue feverish __ medicine.

13th [August]
Still feverish, __ medicine prescribed.

14th [August]
Better.

15th [August]
Letters by [Mr.] Williams [and Rev.] Mr. Maffitt arrived here last Monday [the 12th]. Wrote him [and] sent *Panoplist*. [Rev.] Dr. [Jedidiah] Morse's letter, [and] the first numbers of *Panoplist* [arrive here]. Send Sam[ue]l [Rev. Muir's son] a letter, pair [of] shoes, [and] Vol.1 [and] 2 of *Spectator*.

Note: The Spectator *is a set of essays collected from the extremely popular London periodical of the same name that was produced by Joseph Addison (1672-1719) and Richard Steele (1672-1729). The* Spectator *had been a daily periodical issued in 1711, 1712, and 1714. Several multi-volume editions appear in Britain and the United States during the eighteenth century and early nineteenth century. Recent eight-volume editions appeared in London in 1799 and 1803, and in Philadelphia and Newburyport, Massachusetts in 1803. It is held by the Alexandria Library Company, perhaps through the donation of these volumes. They may have been favorite reading materials of Rev. Muir, whose preaching style was described as "Addisonian," i.e., possessing a direct story-telling approach characterized by accuracy of observation and the occasional use of sly humor (Sprague et al . 1858).*

"*Mr. Williams*" *is Captain Benjamin Williams, an in-law and the husband of Martha Williams. Rev. Muir had visited their family at Middletown, Connecticut in June.*

Rev. Muir makes no record in his diary but he performs a marriage service on Friday, the 16th of August, for Samuel Wheeler and Winifred Winbefield (Brumbaugh 1918-20). Samuel Wheeler is an Alexandria shoemaker.

18th [August, a Sunday]

Forenoon   Exodus 20, 8.9.10.11. [The second sermon in a set of five on the Ten Commandments.]
Do not preach in the afternoon.

19th [August]
Go with Mr. Edmund Lee family to Chantilly.

Notes: Edmund Jennings Lee (1772-1843), a graduate of the College of New Jersey (Princeton University), is a lawyer who serves as a member of Alexandria's Common Council and will serve as Mayor (Lee 1895). The previous month he had delivered the Independence Day address sponsored by the Washington Society to raise tuition funds for the Alexandria Academy.

Mrs. Mary Harper Vowell, wife of Thomas Vowell, dies while Rev. Muir is out of town. He will conduct a memorial service for her on the 1st of September. Her death notice reads, "Departed the transitory life yesterday, Mrs. Mary Vowell, consort of Thomas Vowell, jun. in the 34th year of her age. Her friends and acquaintances are respectfully invited to the funeral, this afternoon at 4 o'clock, from his house in Water street" (Alexandria Daily Advertiser *20 August 1805 p. 3).*

20th [August]
Dine at Mr. Richard B. Lee's [at] Sully.

Note: Richard Bland Lee (1761-1827) is serving in the Virginia House of Delegates. A graduate of the College of New Jersey (Princeton University), he had earlier served as Northern Virginia's first member of the U.S. House of Representatives. He is a brother of Henry Lee, Charles Lee, and Edmund Jennings Lee. His family estate, Sully, is near Chantilly, the estate of Rev. William Maffitt in western Fairfax County (today it is a living history museum managed by the Fairfax County Park Authority; see Gamble 1973).

21st [August]
Have dinner at [Chantilly, the residence of Rev.] Mr. Maffitt.

22nd [August]
Hear [Rev.] Mr. Maffitt examine his [school] boys. Their progress very great.

Note: Rev. Muir's son, Samuel Crichton Muir, attends the school conducted by the Rev. William Maffitt.

23rd [August]
Set off on my return [to Alexandria]. Dine at Mr. James Irvin's [country estate]. Get safe home.

A letter from [Rev.] Dr. [Asbel] Green [has arrived] in answer to mine. Capt. [John] Tucker's family & mother [from] Bermuda at tea. [Rev.] Dr. [Ashbel] Green had received [manuscript for installment] No. 1 Nebuchadnezzar Corrupted – [Rev. Green] questions whether N[ebuchadnezzar] was ever a good man. After Introduction the subject may take them by surprise. [His letter was] dated Bethl[ehem] Pennsylvania 11 Aug[ust] 1805.

25th [August, a Sunday]
Forenoon   Exodus 20, 12.13. [The third sermon in a set of five on the Ten Commandments.]

Afternoon   M[atthe]w 8, 1.2.3.4.

In course of the week [I] wrote No. 2 – Nebuchadnezzar Punished.

Wrote the character of Mrs. Mary Vowell from Mr. Thomas Vowell's observations which he handed me in writing.

Lent Mrs. Edmund <u>Lee</u> [Sarah Lee] Commentary on Old Testament Vol. 1 by __ .

Notes: "Nebuchadnezzar Punished" is the second of four installments of an article of Rev. Muir's being published in General Assembly's Missionary Magazine.

Mary Harper Vowell, wife of Thomas Vowell, had died on the 19th. Rev. Muir conducts a service for her on the 1st of September. Her memorial in the churchyard, which still stands today, includes the words – "in the same lot are deposited four infant children. This monument is erected by the surviving husband as a tribute of love and afflicting remembrance" – a record of the family's personal encounter with the period's distressingly high infant and adult female mortality rates.

Sarah Lee (1775-1837) is the wife of Edmund Jennings Lee and the daughter of Richard Henry Lee (1732-1794).

1st [September, a Sunday]
Forenoon   Mark 9, 2-9. A funeral Sermon for Mrs. Mary Vowell.

Afternoon Ps[alm] 119, 94.

2nd [September]
The [manuscript of installment] No. 2. [on] Nebuchadnezzar [for *General Assembly's Missionary Magazine* is] finished. Added a Ques[tion] – How the writers of the New Testament by Jews wrote in Greek? And also Mrs. Mary Vowell's character [piece is finished; her memorial service was performed a day earlier]. Enclosed the whole to [Rev.] Dr. [Ashbel] Green, w[hich]h I committed to Mr. Thomas Vowell to put in the Post Office & pay the postage. A letter [received] from Miss [Mary] Stewart [at Baltimore], who is well & happy.

5th [September]
Received [*General*] *Assembly* [*Missionary*] *Magazine* No. 8.

7th [September]
[List of amounts paid for several items that are indecipherable]. Received from Philadelphia, the [*General Assembly's Missionary*] *Magazine* to June volume, for which I paid. Two numbers have since been received. Lent Mr. Thomas Vowell 2 numbers of the *Panoplist*.

8th [September, a Sunday]
Forenoon Exodus 20, 14.15.16. Feeling uncommon freedom. [The fourth sermon in a set of five on the Ten Commandments.]
Afternoon Ps[alm] 107, 43.

10th [September]
Wrote [Rev.] Mr. [James] Inglis inviting his aid on the 2nd Lord's Day of October, and [Rev.] Mr. [John] Glendy, reminding him to bring the Presbytery [of Baltimore *Minutes*] Book with him.

11th [September]
Employed preparing an Epitaph for Mrs. Mary Vowell. Consulted for this purpose various Epitaphs among the books in the Library. Compiled from a number what appeared suitable on present occasion.

Mr. and Mrs. Patton [were] thrown out of a [carriage] chair. Mr. [William] P[atton] greatly burdened, Mrs. [Mary] P[atton] thrown into labour.

Note: William Patton, also "Patten," is a local merchant, who is active in the town's public affairs – he signed the petition to incorporate the Alexandria Academy in 1785 and the Meeting House in 1786; signed the petition to free the slave named "Will" in 1792; and is now a member of the St. Andrew's Society and the Friendship Fire Co. He and his wife, Mary Roberdeau Patton, are members of the Meeting House congregation. Rev. Muir will mark her death with a discourse that is published (Muir 1808).

12th [September]
Mrs. [Mary] Patton [delivered] a fine Girl, [this] morning about one.
 Mrs. [Agnes Hepburn] Dundas [delivered in] the afternoon [a] fine Boy.
 Hear of a Mr. [William] Forbes from Jamaica, now in Town, [a man] of Character, [who is] wishing employment as a Teacher.

Notes: William Forbes, a visitor from Jamaica, remains otherwise unidentified. He interacts with Rev. Muir through the end of November, when items he leaves with Muir are sent by ship to him at New York City.

The Patton's "fine Girl" is Selma Blair Patton, daughter of Mary and William Patton, whom Rev. Muir will baptize on the 9th of March 1806.

The Dundas's "fine Boy" is Edward Burnet Dundas, son of Agnes and John Dundas, whom Rev. Muir will baptize on the 9th of February 1806.

13th [September]
Dine at Mr. [Andrew] Jamieson's. Rode with him to his country house. Letter [received] from [Rev.] Mr. [William] Maffitt – will answer on 14th.

14th [September]
Mr. [William] Forbes [of Jamaica] called upon me.

15th [September, a Sunday]
Forenoon   Exodus 20, 17. [Sermon on the final commandment.

At the end of the year, his complete set of commentaries on "The Decalogue" begins appearing in *Panoplist*.]

Afternoon James 5, 14 first clause. ["Are any among you sick?"]

16th [September]

Pay Ja[mes] Kennedy Druggist for bottle of shoe black. Paid 4sh[illings]/6d [reward] for [Rev.] Mr. Maffitt's horse, which had been thought [to be] in his stable. [Pay] Hartshorne for meal [and] Bran. [Rev.] Mr. Maffitt owes me 3 sh[illings], 5$. Sent [him] 3 sh[illings]/. I had owed him 6sh[illings].

Note: Dr. James Kennedy, Sr. (1753-1816), a native of Scotland, is an Alexandria doctor and druggist with a store on King Street. He is a member of the Meeting House congregation.

19th [September]

Hear by Mr. Joseph Riddle that [Rev.] Mr. [James] Inglis [of Baltimore] has been & is sick so that I cannot see him either at the Presbytery or [at Lord's Supper] Sacrament.

On Monday last [I] inclosed my observations on the Decalogue, 8 pages under cover to [Rev.] Dr. Jedidiah Morse, Charleston [Charlestown] near Boston, for the *Panoplist*.

2 numbers left at Mr. Jo[hn] G. Ladd's country house to be forwarded. The Clerk took the Charge thereof in Mr. Ladd's absence, who was at Georgetown. Sent [it] by a vessel that left this after[noon], the 19th [of] October [September].

Notes: Joseph Riddle (1763-1844), a graduate of the College of New Jersey (Princeton University), is an Alexandria merchant, who serves as a director of the Bank of Potomac and on the Board of Health. He was a charter member of the Alexandria Library Company in 1794. He and his wife, Sarah Morrow Kersley Riddle (1782-1810), are both members of the Meeting House congregation, and he serves as a member of the congregation's Church Committee.

Rev. Muir's "The Decalogue" is an eleven-installment set of articles on the Ten Commandments that he contributes to the Panoplist. *They appear between December 1805 and May 1807. He uses the pen name "Philologos" (Lover of The Word) for this and several other publications in popular religious journals.*

John Gardner Ladd (unknown-1819) is a local import merchant and director of the Bank of Potomac. His warehouse is located at Union Street and Prince streets. He and his wife, Elizabeth Ladd, are members of the Meeting House congregation, and he serves the congregation as a member of the Church Committee.

22nd [September, a Sunday]
Forenoon   Daniel 4, 30.31.32.33.
Afternoon M[atthe]w 25, 31.32.33.

23rd [September]
Received a letter from [Rev.] Mr. [Stephen B.] Balch which I answered promising to be at the Presbytery [meeting to be conducted at Bridge-Street (Georgetown) Presbyterian Church, Friday and Saturday, 4 and 5 October] & [to] continue [to stay in Georgetown] until after the L[ord's] day [on the 6th to preach at the Bridge-Street (Georgetown) Presbyterian Church]. The meeting [of Presbytery to begin] on the 4th [of] October.

24th [September]
Wrote by Mr. William Forbes an introductory letter to [Rev.] Messrs. [James] Inglis and [Samuel] Knox, [at] Baltimore. [I was] left with [his] telescope, microscope, galvanic instruments to be disposed of at his order.

Notes: Rev. Dr. James Inglis (1777-1820) is minister of Baltimore's First Presbyterian Church.

Rev. Samuel Knox is an ordained Presbyterian minister then serving as President of Baltimore College.

25th [September]
A full [midweek evening prayer-worship service] meeting [on] Wednesday. [Rev.] Mr. [Conrad] Spence with us, who with Dr. Dykes breakfasted with me.

On 26th Mr. J. Wilson called on me. [He] sets off for London on Saturday.

27th [September]
Wrote Mr. [John] Mills of London and sent [letter] w[ith] Mr. Wilson who promised to take charge th[ere]of.

29th [**September, a Sunday**]
Forenoon   Daniel 4, 34.35.36.37.
Afternoon   [Rev.] Mr. Spence preached. He is a judicious well-informed man, but from want of accurate study, [his] Sermons are tedious & come by a circuitous rout[e] to the point, which renders w[ha]t [he] says less impressive than otherwise it w[oul]d be. He has a clear idea of the truth, & __ out a torrent of substantial truths.

Notes: Rev. Muir does not note that he performs a funeral service on the 2nd of October for six-year old Andrew Fleming, who died of fever. He is a son of Andrew Fleming (1759-1820), a local builder and member of the St. Andrew's Society, who served in the Revolutionary War. Andrew and Catherine Steele Fleming, are members of the Meeting House. Nicholas Cresswell, who referred to Meeting House Presbyterians as a "set of rebellious scoundrels" when he visited Alexandria in the 1770s, lodged with the Flemings (Cresswell 1924, Sengel 1973, Thompson 1989).

Rev. Conrad Spence, formerly with the Presbyterian congregation at Cabin John, Maryland and now without a charge, has been provided several opportunities by Rev. Muir to preach at the Meeting House.

Rev. Muir does not record in his diary that he performs a marriage service for Samuel Endicott and Polley Call on the first of October (Brumbaugh 1918-20).

4th [**October**]   Go to Georgetown [District of Columbia] to meet[ing of] the Presbytery. Lodge at Mrs. Peter's [at Georgetown].

Note: Rev. Muir serves as moderator of these sessions of the Presbytery of Baltimore, which convene at Bridge-Street (Georgetown) Presbyterian Church on Friday and Saturday, the 4th and 5th of October. He preaches to presbytery on the first day of its sessions from Isaiah Chapter 1, Verses 10-19. Presbytery's business sessions are largely devoted to discussion of ways to fulfill the demand for ministers at congregations lacking installed clergy.

6th [**October, a Sunday**]   At Georgetown [District of Columbia]. Morning   Dan[ie]l 4, 34.35.36.37. [Rev.] Mr. [Stephen B.] Balch dispersed the Sacrament [of the Lord's Supper].
Returned in the even[in]g to Alexandria.

Note: Rev. Muir is guest preaching at the Bridge-Street (Georgetown) Presbyterian Church.

7th [October]
Received a letter from [Rev.] Mr. [James] Inglis [of Baltimore] who is [in] better [health]. [He] has received no injury from his sickness but [suffered the] loss of flesh, strength, & appetite. [He] had seen Mr. [William] Forbes, and introduced him to Mr. [Christopher] Johnston [also of Baltimore].

Received [*General*] *Assembly* [*Missionary*] *Magazine* No. 9.

Have finished [writing installments] No. 3 [and] No. 4 [of] Nebuchadnezzar [for *General Assembly's Missionary Magazine*]. Inclosed them to [Rev.] Dr. [Ashbel] Green [in Philadelphia]. Put them in the Post office. Payed the postage __ .

8th [October]
Still confined.

9th [October]
Confined [to] residence [the parsonage on Royal Street]. Ill for the four past nights. Write out *Minutes* of Presbytery [meeting] during [from] last April. Confined the rest of week.

Rec[ei]v[e]d Dr. Price's Sermon's on the Gospel.

13th [October, a Sunday]
Unable to attend Service.

14th, 15th, and 16th [October]
Read [Donald] Campbell's Adventures of a Journey by Land to India, [*General*] *Assembly* [*Missionary*] *Magazine*, [and] Watson's Tracts. Finish Dr. Price's ac[count of the] Gospel. His observations convince me of ministerial forbearance, but find no reason to depart from doctrines taught our Church. Difficulties attached [to] some [of] the doctrines, nor is his scheme free from difficulties. There is certainly more agreed [to] than many of them will admit. Al[l who] but see darkly thro' a glass ought to be diffident of th[em]selves, claiming promise to __ in the __ . "They shall be taught of G[od]." [John 6:45].

Notes: "Adventures" is the then-popular literary work by Donald Campbell, A Journey Over Land to India: Partly by a Route Never

Gone Before by Any European. *It was first published in London by Cullen and Co. in 1795, with numerous later editions.*

Rev. Muir received the six volumes of Watson's A Collection of Theological Tracts *(1791) on the 15th of April.*

Rev. Muir makes no record here, but he performs a marriage service for William Martin and Mary Woodrow on the 17th of October (Brumbaugh 1918-20). William Martin is a blacksmith with shop located on Alfred Street.

18th [October]

Received 2 sets of No. 3, [and] 4 of the *Panoplist*, one for [Rev.] Mr. Maffitt, one my own.   24 [word crossed out], 12 sheets, 2 [word crossed out]. Sent my set to Mr. Tho[ma]s Vowell who is sick.   Received from him yesterday No. 1 [&] No. 2.   Still confined tho' better.

Mr. [Elisha Cullen] Dick sent me "Shakespeare Illustrated[;] or, the Novels and Histories on Which the Plays of Shakespeare are Founded, Collected & Translated from Original Authors with Critical Remarks, 2 vol[umes] by author [of The] Female Quixote, &c. Mrs. [Charlotte] Lennox" [published in London, 1753-54].

Sent Mr. And[re]w Jamieson [copies of] *Panoplist* Nos. 1, 2, 3, 4. Got No. __ , which belonged to [Rev.] Mr. Maffitt.

20th [October, a Sunday]
Forenoon   Luke 8, 43-49.
Afternoon   Isaiah 1, 10-19.

23rd [October]
Mr. <u>Tygen</u> from Baltimore called upon me.

27th [October, a Sunday]
Morning   Ps[alm] 22, 27.   Action Sermon.   Dispensed the Sacrament [of the Lord's Supper].
Afternoon   [Rev.] Mr. [David] Wiley preached a good discourse.

Notes: "Action Sermon" refers to the sermon delivered in conjunction with the service of the Lord's Supper. Late September-early October is one of the four times of the year that the Lord's Supper is commonly served among Presbyterian congregations during this period (see also diary entry at 31 March).

Rev. Muir does not record in his diary that he performs a marriage service for John Parker and Mary Hill this same day (Brumbaugh 1918-20). John Parker is an Alexandria blacksmith.

28th [October]
[Rev.] Mr. [David] Wiley [visits] here. Dine with him at Mr. [Joseph] Riddle's. See him on board packet [boat] for Charlestown [South Carolina]. I write [Rev.] Mr. [Isaac Stockton] Keith of Charleston on his behalf, as he wished to go as a teacher to the Southward. Left my letter with Mr. Riddle.

Note: Rev. Dr. Isaac Stockton Keith (1755-1813) served the Meeting House immediately prior to the arrival of Rev. Muir, from 1780 to 1788. He now serves the Independent [Reformed] Church at Charleston, South Carolina. He had returned to Alexandria to visit and serve as guest preacher at the Meeting House in November of 1802.

30th [October]
Receive a letter from the <u>William Forbes</u> from <u>Newcastle</u>, Delaware [posted on] 26 October. [He] had been treated well by [Rev.] Mr. [James] Inglis & Mr. [Christopher] Johnston's family [at Baltimore]. [He is] Disappointed [at] not hav[in]g received his Baggage. [He is now] on his way to N[ew]York, [and] probably to Louisiana, [with] directions to be afterward communicated with respect to the th[in]g[s] of his [being] under my care.

Note: Rev. Muir performs a marriage service for Henry Lyles and Mary Davis on the 31st of October without making note of it in his diary (Brumbaugh 1918-20).

2nd [November]
Received a letter from [Rev.] Dr. Sam[ue]l Miller dated Newark [New Jersey], w[here he had] fled from New York [City], wishing [requesting] a keg of Mr. [Andrew] Jamieson's crackers.

3rd [November, a Sunday]
Forenoon Romans 13-14 first clause.
Afternoon Ps[alm] 22, 27. 2nd sermon [on this passage; and] Hebrews 11, 6. 1st [portion of] sermon [on this passage; two others to follow.]

5th [November]
Received [*General*] *Assembly* [*Missionary*] *Magazine* No. 10 [for] 6 cents. Read it. Make some calls. Meet the [Church] Committee [of the Meeting House] at Mr. [Thomas] Vowell's.

6th [November]
Between 20 [and] 30 at[tend] the [Wednesday] evening meeting, the service impressive.

10th [November, a Sunday]
Morning   Heb[rews] 11, 6. 2nd sermon [on this passage].
Afternoon Heb[rews] 11, 6. 3rd sermon [on this passage].

13th [November]
Purchase at Mr. [James] Wilson's vendue [auction], a escritoire [for] 12$50/100 [with] a marble slab on the top. Some repairs wanting. Left [it to be repaired] with Jo[hn] Muir.
   Mr. Edmund Lee has returned Vol. 2 of Commentary [on] O[ld] T[estament]. [I] received Vol. 3. [Give] Mr. [Jonathan] Swift [*General Assembly's Missionary*] *Magazine* – No. 9 & 10. [Give] Mrs. [Jane Perry] Hill – No. 1. [Give] Old Mr. [James] Douglass – Nos. 1 [and] 2 pamphlets which I had received from Mr. [Andrew] Jamieson.

Notes: Rev. Muir purchases an escritoire, a writing desk, from the auction of goods from James Wilson's estate. Wilson died on the 9th of July. Rev. Muir leaves his new purchase for repairs with John Muir, "one of Alexandria's most famous [early] furniture makers"(Kabler 1957, Minter-Dowd 1979). The escritoire will remain in the Muir family through Rev. Muir's death.

John Muir (1770-1815) is one of several Muirs living in Alexandria. It is not known if he is directly related to the Rev. Muir. John Muir and his wife, Mary Muir, are both members of the Meeting House congregation.

Jane Perry Hill is the wife of Laurence Hill, who owns a local cooperage. The family resides at 209 South Lee Street. They are both members of the Meeting House congregation, and he serves the congregation as a member of the Church Committee.

James Douglass (unknown-1811) is a merchant, with business establishment on King Street, who was a charter member of the Alexandria Library Company. He and his wife, Mary, are members of the Meeting House congregation.

15th [November]
Letter from Sam[ue]l [Rev. Muir's son]. [He] is well. His leg on mend & hand [also].

17th [November, a Sunday]
Morning   1 Peter 5, 8. 1st sermon [on this passage].
Afternoon   Luke 22, 31.32.

18th [November]
Received [issue] No. 5 [of the] *Panoplist*. [Paid] 14 cents. One for [Rev.] Mr. Maffitt, one my own.

19th [November]
With Judge [Nicholas] Fitzhugh, [I] visit the poor school [the tuition-free portion of the Alexandria Academy]. [It] improves.
  A letter from Mr. [John] Mills [of] London [arrived] by Capt. Boyne via Charleston. 25-2 [indecipherable monetary denomination]. __ arrived Mr. Carr's [on] 1 August. [It] had [been] sent 1st July. A [Rev.] Mr. [Robert] Young has succeeded [Rev.] Dr. [Henry] Hunter [in London]. Mr. S__ gone to Leath [in northwestern England].
  A Jew preaches Christ with clearness and __ [from the] date [of] his C[onversion], [on] 22 August.
  Nary a day in the month has not passed without rain. The necessities [of] life double __ . Clothes __ . Each minds his own business. Politics seldom mentioned. The weather prevented go[in]g abroad. I'd sleep __ . Messrs [John] Dunlop [and Samuel] Craig particularly remembered.
  [Rev.] Mr. [Joseph] <u>Washburn</u> with his lady from Farmington, Connecticut called upon us. He is in decline [and] on his way southward. [They] lodge with attendants with a Dr. <u>Abernathy</u>.

Notes: Judge Nicholas Fitzhugh (unknown-1814) was appointed as an Assistant Judge of the Alexandria Circuit Court by President Thomas Jefferson in 1803. He also serves as a trustee of the Alexandria Academy, and resides at 220 North Washington Street (now known as Lloyd House).

  Rev. Dr. Henry Hunter (1741-1802), a cousin of Rev. Muir's, had served as minister of the Scots Church (Church of Scotland) at London Wall in the City of London from 1771 to 1802. Rev. Muir completed his divinity training with Rev. Hunter, and then served as an assistant minister with him from 1776 to 1781. Rev. Dr. Robert Young (1777-1813) served as minister of the Scots Church from 1803 until his death in 1813.

The name of the Jew who had converted to Christianity and is now proselytizing in the name of Christ is not known. He presumably addressed Alexandrians during the week at a local congregation.

John Dunlop, also "John Dunlap" (1756-1806), is an Alexandria merchant, who had served in the Revolutionary War; had signed the Meeting House's incorporation petition in 1786; and was a charter member of the Alexandria Library Company. He and his wife, Elizabeth Dunlop (1748-1812), are both members of the Meeting House congregation.

Rev. Joseph Washburn, a Congregational Church clergyman since 1795, served as minister of the Congregational congregation in Farmington, Connecticut, until his health declined earlier in the year. He stops at Alexandria while journeying to Charleston, South Carolina in search of a more salubrious climate. He will perish while sailing from Norfolk to Charleston and be buried at sea on the 25th of December.

20th [November]
Wet. [Only] a few attend [midweek] evening [service].

21st [November]
[Rev.] Mr. [James] Inglis wrote letter that was dated 17th.

22nd [November]
Mr. Leher called upon me.

23rd [November]
[Rev.] Mr. [Joseph] Washburn still here; unable to proceed.

24th [November, a Sunday]
Forenoon   Hebrews 13, 1.2.3. and Deut[eronomy] 10, 19.
  [Preach] before St. Andrew's Society; 33$ [received in donations]. Wet.
Afternoon   1 Tim[othy] 4, 8. 2 Cor[inthians] 13, 13.

Note: Members of Alexandria's St. Andrew's Society, established during the 1780s as a charitable association, join with Rev. Muir's congregation for worship each year on St. Andrew's Day, the first Sunday in Advent. Monetary contributions received at the service are used to assist Alexandrians in need.

25th [November]
[Rev.] Mr. [Joseph] Washburn at Mr. Joseph Riddle's request went to his house.
  Dr. Abernathy lodges at Dr. Saunderson's.

26th [November]
A letter [arrived] from [Rev.] Dr. [Ashbel] Green dated 7th Nov[ember]. [He] had received Nebuchadnezzar [manuscript for publication in *General Assembly's Missionary Magazine* on] Nov. 4. [He was] absent when my letter arrived. The insertion [of this installment in the *General Assembly's Missionary Magazine* will be] delayed until next Number. [Rev.] Mr. Joseph Washburn has represented to him the list of men & ministers.

27th [November]
Was 30 [that attended] at our [midweek evening prayer-worship] meeting.

29th [November]
Give Mr. [Thomas] Vowell No. 5 of the *Panoplist*.

30th [November]
A letter from Samuel [Rev. Muir's son and] request from [Rev.] Mr. Maffitt borrowing __ and No. 5 *Panoplist*.
  Sent [to] Mr. James Patton's store every th[in]g left with me belonging to Mr. [William] Forbes, to be sent to New York [City], by a vessel that sails on Monday, except the Galvanic Trough & two __ on Galvanism.
  Received a letter from Revd. W[illia]m Hill introducing the Revd. George A. Baxter, rector of Washington Academy, [at] Rockbridge County [Virginia].

Notes: Rev. Dr. William Hill serves the Presbyterian Church at Winchester, Virginia.
  Rev. Dr. George A. Baxter (1771-1831) is a Presbyterian minister who serves as President of Liberty Hall (today's Washington and Lee University) from 1799 to 1829. Following his presidency at Liberty Hall, Rev. Baxter will join the faculty of Union Theological Seminary as Professor of Theology. Union Theological

Seminary, will be established in 1812 at Farmville, Virginia (it is today's Union Presbyterian Seminary, located at Richmond).

*Rev. Muir does not note in his diary that he attends a business meeting of Alexandria's St. Andrew's Society on this evening and is re-elected to serve as the Society's chaplain (*Alexandria Daily Advertiser *2 December 1805 p. 2).*

1st [December, a Sunday]
Morning 1 Pet[er] 5, 8. 2nd sermon [on this passage].
Afternoon and evening.

[Preaching is Rev.] Mr. [George A.] Baxter from Rockbridge [County, Virginia] who presides over Washington Academy – a deliberate, judicious, impressive preacher; a fine countenance & melodious voice; nothing rehearsed; goes on from one hand to another without a pause – or breaking pace at [the] conclusion of the one and commencement of the other.

2nd [December]
Wrote by [Rev.] Mr. Baxter to [Rev.] Mr. [Stephen B.] Balch and [to Rev. Mr. David] Wiley and [to] The Hon[ora]ble George Clinton Vice President.

Note: George Clinton (1739-1812) serves as Vice President of the United States under both Presidents Jefferson and Madison, from 1805 to 1812.

3rd [December]
Received from Mr. Tho[ma]s Vowell 10$ for [Rev.] Mr. [Joseph] Washburn.

4th [December]
From Mr. [John] Dunlop 20$.

5th [December]
Pay Mr. Gerd's sister 2$ in part what due Mr. Gerd.

6th [December]
[*General Assembly's Missionary*] *Magazine* No. 11 [arrives]. [Pay] 6 cents.

7th [December]

[Rev.] Mr. Joseph Washburn sailed [for Charleston], gave 35$ to him from various friends.

8th [December, a Sunday]
Forenoon 1 Pet[er] 5, 8. 3rd sermon [on this passage].
Afternoon Matthew 4, 1-8.

9th [December]
Set off with Mr. [Andrew] Jamieson [elder at Meeting House] & [Rev.] Mr. [William] Hill for Chantilly [the estate of the Rev. William Maffitt at] ab[ou]t 11 [a.m]. Arrived at ab[out] sunset. [We] did not stop by the road. At supper [I] stayed with the family. [I] fell attempting to get out and to the ground. Recovered in a few minutes.

10th [December]
Ride to Sully, [the country] seat of Richard Bland Lee, Esq. Return [to Chantilly] for dinner. Dine at Sully on 11th with [Rev.] Mr. [William] Maffitt, [Mr.] [Andrew] Jamieson, [Rev.] Mr. [William] Hill, at 8 [p.m.]

Set off on 12th [to] home. Dine at James Irvin, Esq. at Alex[andri]a a little after sunset on the 12th. Dine at Mr. [William James] Hall's [on 13th]. Tea at Capt. Ball's. __ for study.

Note: William James Hall (1762-1810), originally from Ireland, is a local merchant with a store on Union Street. He is a member of the Meeting House congregation. His wife, Nancy Grace Craig Hall (1780-1798), who died of complications during child birth in 1798, was interred at the Meeting House Burial Ground.

14th [December]
Gave a check for 20$. 100 segars [cigars for] 9 [shillings]. Sent Samuel [a] c[op]y of Dawson[']s Greek Testament [and Rev.] Mr. Maffitt the 4 remaining volumes of Mosheim.

Notes: The "4 remaining volumes of Mosheim" refers to volumes of the six-volume work by the German theologian Johann Lorenz Mosheim (1693-1755) that Rev. Muir shares with his nearby colleague Rev. Maffitt – An Ecclesiastical History: Antient (sic) and Modern, From the Birth of Christ, to the Beginning of the Present Century; In Which the Rise, Progress, and Variations of Church Power are Considered in their Connexion with the State of Learn-

ing and Philosophy, and the Political History of Europe During That Period, by the Late Learned John Lawrence Mosheim; Translated from the Original Latin, and Accompanied with Notes and Chronological Tables by Archibald Maclaine, D.D. *The first American edition was published in Philadelphia in 1797-98.*

"Dawson's Greek Testament" sent to Samuel is no doubt the handy New Testament of Our Lord and Saviour *(Oxford), issued in numerous versions from the 1780s throughout this period by W. Dawson at London.*

15th [December, a Sunday]
Morning   Heb[rews] 8, 10.11.12.
Afternoon Heb[rews] 4, 16. [First sermon on this passage].

16th [December]
[Attend] Alexandria's Theatre Trial of J[ohn] Atkins Burford. Court adjourned until tomorrow at 9 o'clock, a witness b[ein]g absent.

Received for myself and [Rev.] Mr. Maffitt [two copies of the] *Panoplist* No. 6, [costing] 14 cents. Lent Mr. Ricketts [*General Assembly's Missionary*] *Magazine* No. 11. Lent Mr. [Thomas] Vowell No. 6 [of the] *Panoplist.*

*Note: John Burford is being tried for robbing and wounding John Peter, clerk for the Bank of Columbia, an act that occurred just outside Alexandria on the 30th of July (Rev. Muir recorded his reactions to the robbery, which involved a member of his congregation assisting the wounded John Peter in an entry on 31 July). The trial continues into the next day. The "Theatre Trial" terminology used by Rev. Muir comes from the trial having been moved from the local court chambers to the Spring-Green Theatre "for the convenience of the Court" in accommodating a large public audience. The trial has become a very public contest over the administration of justice (*Alexandria Daily Advertiser *14 December 1805 p. 3). The trial continues for another day.*

Mr. Ricketts is either David Ricketts (1765-1831) or his brother John Thomas Ricketts (1754-1821). Both families are members of the Meeting House congregation; David will become an elder in the Presbyterian Church in 1816.

17th [December]

At the court all day, hearing the pleading by Messrs. Jones, Young, __ , Swan and __. Return home la[te] in the morning.

*Note: The outcome of the trial's proceedings are briefly reported in the local newspaper – "The Circuit Court of the District of Columbia [held in Alexandria], has been engaged for the last two days on the trial of John A. Burford, for the robbery and attempt to murder, Mr. Peter, of the Bank of Columbia, in June [actually July] last; and this morning the jury brought in the verdict of Not Guilty" (*Alexandria Daily Advertiser *18 December 1805 p. 3).*

In spite of being found not guilty, John Burford remains confined in the Alexandria jail by local Justices of the Peace through the 28th of December. He appeals his confinement to the federal District Court, and to the U.S. Supreme Court, where justices find unanimously in his favor that "the warrant of [his] commitment was illegal for want of stating some good cause certain, supported by oath... [and ordered that] the prisoner is discharged" (Cranch 1812 Vol. III, pp. 448-453).

18th [December]

Messrs Page [and] Roberts waited upon me requesting, from [Masonic] Lodge No. 22, my services on the L[ord's] day in a Charity Sermon.

In the evening, 40 at society [i.e., the group of congregation members that attend the midweek service].

Note: Services such as this Charity Sermon sponsored by Alexandria's Masonic Lodge No. 22 are major civic events that come to include significant participation by the general populace of the town. Local residents are drawn into participating in such events by a very public street procession. The procession for this particular event gathers at Market Square and parades south on Fairfax Street to the Presbyterian Meeting House. Notices for public events such as this appear for days in local newspapers. Ones for this event read – "CHARITY SERMON At the request of the Brethren of Lodge No. 22, and the anticipation of the festival of St. John the Evangelist, a CHARITY SERMON will be preached by the Rev. Mr. Muir, at the Presbyterian Church, on Sunday morning next [22 December]. The members of Lodge No. 22, are requested to assemble at their hall at 10 o'clock A.M. on that day, to move in procession to church. Brethren of other Lodges are respectfully invited to attend. Note–There will be no service at the

*Episcopal church on the morning of that day." (*Alexandria Daily Advertiser *19 December 1805 p. 3 and 20 December 1805 p. 4).*

It is a measure of the civic importance of this event that public notice is given that the upcoming Sunday worship service at the Episcopal Church will not be conducted. Most denominations cancel their own worship service to enable members to join in the larger community service (Brockett and Uhler 1899, Davis 1986).

19th [December]

Attended at Mr. [Andrew] Jamieson [elder at the Meeting House for] the distribution [of] poor money.

20th [December]

A letter from [Rev.] Mr. [Joseph] Washburn. [He] had arrived at Norfolk in 29 hours & intended to proceed by land to [Charleston] S[outh] Carolina.

Hear of a victory over the Combined Fleets. L[or]d Nelson lost his life.

Notes: The Rev. Joseph Washburn, a Congregational minister from Connecticut, had arrived at Alexandria in mid-November and left for Charleston in early December (diary entries from 19 November through 3 December). Contrary to the message he conveys to Rev. Muir, Washburn decides to travel from Norfolk by ship, and dies on Christmas Day while still at sea.

Rev. Muir's hearing "of a victory over the Combined Fleets" refers to the victory at the Battle of Trafalgar off the southwest coast of Spain on the 21st of October of the British Royal Navy's fleet of twenty-seven ships, led by Admiral Lord Nelson, over the Combined Fleet of thirty-three French and Spanish ships. Admiral Lord Nelson was killed in that engagement. A detailed account of the engagement appeared in the Alexandria Daily Advertiser *for 20 December 1805.*

22nd [December, a Sunday]

   Forenoon   Luke 10, 30-38. A very great assembly [of members of Masonic] Lodge – 22 present.

   Afternoon Heb[rews] 4, 16. 2nd sermon [on this passage].

Collected in the morning 84$.

Note: Money collected at public charity sermons sponsored by the Alexandria-Washington Masonic Lodge No. 22 that are con-

ducted twice a year in celebration of the festival days of St. John the Evangelist, on the 27th of December, and of St. John the Baptist, on the 24th of June, supports those in need among the general citizenry of Alexandria. Note that "the very great assembly" of Lodge members that Rev. Muir refers to as attending the service numbers twenty-two persons.

25th [Christmas Day, a Wednesday]
Forenoon Is[aiah] 9,6

Not a quorum remained [of congregation members for a meeting following worship service] to choose a [Church] Committee, [so] the former [members] remain [in office], of course.

Dine at Mr. [John] Richard's, with Miss [Anne] Donaldson Fairfax, Mr. [Joseph] Riddle, B___, Saunderson, Miss Mark, N___. Dr. Saunderson had been at Chantilly for James Riddle, who by an accident cut off entirely two joints of his middle fingers of the left hand.

Notes: Rev. Muir preaches on a text from the Old Testament prophet Isaiah on the coming kingdom of God, and not on a New Testament text describing the birth of Christ. Christmas, like Easter, is not celebrated in public worship at the Meeting House in anything like the manner that will emerge in the twentieth century (Melton 1967, Thompson 1963-73, Rhys 1982, Nelson 2001). Like many others, Presbyterians celebrate Christmas privately within the family. Well into the nineteenth century, Christmas Day at the Meeting House is most likely to consist of a brief service and a meeting of congregation members to select persons to serve on the Church Committee for the upcoming year, followed by a meeting of the new committee members.

Dr. John Richards (1767-1843) is an Alexandria physician who trained at the universities of Glasgow and Edinburgh. He and his wife, Jane Richards, are members of the Meeting House congregation, and he serves as a member of the Church Committee.

James Riddle is believed to be a son of Joseph and Frances Riddle who is studying with the Rev. William Maffit at Chantilly along with Samuel Muir.

Rev. Muir makes no record in his diary but he also performs a marriage service for George Ashford and Susana Compton on this day (Brumbaugh 1918-20).

The Alexandria Daily Advertiser *does not appear on Christmas Day. It had noted in its Christmas Eve edition that "Tomorrow being Christmas, this paper will not be issued 'till Thursday next."*

27th [December]

Mr. Francis L. Lee allows <u>Delly</u> to remain [with us for] another year. Jane [Muir, Rev. Muir's oldest daughter] at the Mason's Ball. Have since Monday had no servant but Delly & the [Meeting House] sexton.

Notes: Delly is one of several female servants in the Muir household during the year.

Francis Lightfoot Lee II (1782-1850) is a son of Richard Henry Lee (1732-1794) and the namesake of his uncle, Francis Lightfoot Lee (1734-1797). A recent graduate of Harvard College he is now studying law there. He will present a public address in Alexandria sponsored by the Washington Society in 1807.

29th [December, a Sunday]

Forenoon   James 4, 14.
Afternoon   Is[aiah] 57, 15.

31st [December]

Receive a letter from [Rev.] Mr. Mattson of Bermuda.

Note: Rev. Enoch Mattson (1771-1831) is the minister of Christ Church (Church of Scotland) at Warwick, Bermuda. He followed Rev. Muir in this position. Originally a Methodist, he was ordained to serve as a minister in the Presbyterian Church in the U.S.A. as the result of Rev. Muir's intervention on his behalf. He trained with Rev. Muir and was ordained by the Presbytery of Baltimore at services conducted at the Meeting House on the 16th of April 1793.

Part III. APPENDICES

A. Title Page and Handwritten Notes Appearing on End Pages of Diary

[*Title Page.*]

The Town and Country Almanac
for the Year of Our Lord, 1805.
Being the first after Leap-Year; and the twenty-ninth of
American Independence.
Calculated for the Meridian of Washington City
Containing, the rising, setting, places and eclipses of the Sun and
Moon; Longitude of her ascending Node; The geocentric places
and aspects of the planets; The rising, setting and southing of the
most conspicuous planets and fixed Stars; The equation of Time;
Passage of Alloth over the meridian; Sun's declination; Judgment
of weather; Table shewing the value of Dollars, from 1 to 10,000;
Table of Weights, and value of Coins; Table of Interest, at
6 percent; List of roads, and a general Tide Table for the
United States.
Also, A Variety of Selections, Instructive and Entertaining,
in Prose and Verse; The astronomical calculations
by Abraham Shoemaker of New-York.

. . .

Printed for, and sold by Robert and John Gray,
Alexandria

[*Handwritten notes appearing on the first originally blank end page.*]

21 Sept 1936 W. H. Biggs $2.30 exc.

For a __ . A __ made of __ & __ .
Direction[s]
Mr. John Mills at Mr. Carr's, Grocer
St. Paul's Church Yard, London—See Nov[ember] 19.

AY326 A3 T71 1805

Notes: The initial entry is in a style of penmanship that appears nowhere else in the volume. It seems to indicate that the diary was purchased by W. H. Biggs for $2.30 in September of 1936.

The incomplete entry that begins "For a __ ... " is a note, jotted down by Rev. Muir, that makes reference to a diary entry that appears on the 19th of November when he received a letter from London. He interacted with John Mills of London several times during the year.

"AY326 A3 T71 1805" is the Library of Virginia call number for the diary.

[*Handwritten notes appearing on second originally blank end page.*]

State[ment of Financial] Ac[coun]t [as of] 29th Jan[uar]y 1805 –
Mr. Sam[ue]l Craig, for a piece of linen at 6£ per yard [followed by indecipherable amounts].
Only balance of [indecipherable amounts]. Robt. Welman segars [cigars] $5.50 [Rev. Muir pays this amount in reimbursement for a gift made to him; see entry at the 12th of March].
General [assistance] for Jane [Muir]'s schooling. Paid by Jan[uar]y on 7th March. Mary [Muir]'s schooling payed up until 10th Dec[ember]. Last $5 a quarter on 7th March __ . Payed 5$ due, 10th [of] March. Jane [Muir] payed $10 a quarter [on] 18 May. 10$ pd.
Miss [Mary] Stewart's [and] Mary [Muir]'s passage f[ro]m Bermuda to Norfolk – Capt. William W. Newbold. 25$ pd.
Capt. [Samuel] Welman Bermuda, no specific sum, but a debt of gratitude.
Find by a letter of sale – the a __ of tobacco, 8' of white Thread, needles, pins will be reasonable, by first appointments __ w[it]h a B[arre]l [of] flour.
I know of no other demand upon me –

	$
Have in Bank _ _ _ _ _ _ _	90
In Eagles _ _ _ _ _ _ _ _ _	40
[In] Notes, 15, half eagles, 5 _	20
[In] Dollars _ _ _ _ _ _ _ _	14
[In] Small change _ _ _ _ _	10
	174

Notes: Samuel Craig (1763-1808) is an Alexandria merchant, member of the town's Common Council, and charter member and treasurer of the Alexandria Library Company. He and his wife, Joanna Craig (1756-1806) are members of the Meeting House congregation, and he serves as treasurer of the congregation's Church Committee.

Robert Welman is an in-law of Rev. Muir's from Bermuda who was living in New York City in 1805.

Jane Wardlaw Muir (1788-1862), who is seventeen years of age, was the firstborn child of the Rev. James and Elizabeth Welman Muir. She is one of three daughters.

Mary Wardlaw Muir (1794-1860), is the family's second daughter, who spent a portion of the year in Bermuda.

Mary Stewart is the daughter of one of two Stewart families in the Meeting House congregation, either John Ainsworth Stewart and his wife, Elizabeth Dunlap Stewart, or James A. Stewart and his wife, Jane Stewart.

Captain Samuel Welman, of Bermuda, is Rev. Muir's father-in-law.

[*Handwritten notes appearing on the third originally blank end page.*]

Debts
Mr. Stevenson doing some thing to __. Paid.
  Supply [ministers] for my pulpit [while I am attending meetings of the General Association of Congregational Churches in Connecticut] in –
  June
2nd [Sunday, Rev.] Stephen Balch
3rd [Sunday, Rev. John] Brackenridge
4th [Sunday, Rev. David] Wiley
5th [Sunday, Rev.] William Williamson
  July
1st [Sunday, Rev. James] Inglis.

Notes: These are notes that Rev. Muir has jotted down to serve as reminders. The Reverends Stephen B. Balch, William Maffitt, David Wiley, and John Brackenridge are appointed supplies to the pulpit of the Meeting House at the General Assembly of the Presbyterian Church in the U.S.A. in May 1805. Though appointed to serve, the Rev. William Maffitt will apparently not be available, but the other clergymen have apparently agreed to specific dates to supply the Meeting House pulpit while Rev. Muir is away. (Presbyterian Church in the U.S.A. 1847).

Rev. Dr. Stephen Bloomer Balch (1747-1833) serves the Bridge-Street (Georgetown) Presbyterian Church in the District of Columbia from 1780 to 1833.

Rev. John Brackenridge served the St. Andrew's Presbyterian Church at Washington, D.C., a congregation that eventually joined with other congregations to form Washington's National Presbyterian Church. Rev. Brackenridge also serves as Chaplain for members of both the U.S. House of Representatives and the U.S. Senate. In 1813, Rev. Muir preached at his installation as minister of First Presbyterian Church at Washington, D.C.

Rev. David Wiley (unknown-1813) is a Presbyterian minister who headed the Columbian Academy, a private classical school in Georgetown, D.C. He was a graduate of the College of New Jersey (Princeton University) and had served congregations in Pennsylvania as well as the Hyattsville (Maryland) Presbyterian Church prior to moving to Georgetown in 1802. He preached at the Meeting House several times during the year.

Rev. William Williamson (1764-1848) serves the Presbyterian congregation in Middleburg, Virginia, where he also headed a school from 1804 to 1848. He was born in Scotland, where he was educated at the University of Edinburgh and had practiced law prior to emigrating to the United States around 1790. He was ordained as a minister in the Presbyterian Church by the Presbytery of Winchester in 1793.

Rev. Dr. James Inglis (1777-1820) serves the First Presbyterian Church at Baltimore and is another close associate of Rev. Muir's in the Presbytery of Baltimore (Smith 1899). Rev. Muir officiated at the wedding service of Rev. Inglis and Jane S. Johnston in 1802.

[Handwritten notes appearing on the fourth originally blank end page.]

Mal[achi] 4, 2. "The sun of righteousness shall arise with healing in his wings."
I lately met with an explanation of this metaphor so descriptive of the Redeemer's character, which was much more agreeable and satisfactory to me, than I am persuaded it must be to the readers of the magazine. An English Divine informed from his son residing at Smyrna [on the Aegean coast of modern Turkey], of a wind which there begins to blow at the rising of the Sun, so salubrious in its effects as to be generally spoken of under the name of the Doctor. It occurred to him that the "wings of the wind" was a

Scripture phrase, and that Malachi might have known the healing virtues of the wind mentioned by his Son concluded, that the Prophet from Greece called this image of the Sun rising on the wings of salvation's winds representing the benefits men receive from the knowledge and efficacy of Christ, by the benefit which they receive from the rising sun all __ with ~~refreshing~~ breezes – which refresh the spirits, and brace the nervous system.

B. Bible Texts of Sermons by Rev. Dr. Muir during 1805, in the Order Delivered

Malachi 4, 2
Luke 13, 6-10
2 Peter 1, 16
Hebrews 1, 1
2 Peter 1, 16
1 Samuel 1, 17-18
Luke 7, 35–
James 4, 8
John 8, 47–
1 Corinthians 7, 29-31
Psalm 107, 43
Luke 20, 27-39
Matthew 6, 13
Luke 20, 27-39
Matthew 13, 24-31
Psalm 110
Matthew 28, 18-20
Acts 3, 22 and Hebrews 12, 25
Luke 7, 11-19
Philippians 2, 8
Philippians 2, 9-11
Acts 11, 26
Matthew 28, 20
Acts 11, 26
2 Corinthians 5, 14-15 and 1 Timothy 3, 16
Numbers 6, 22-27 and 2 Corinthians 13, 13
Psalm 122, 1
Numbers 6, 22-27
2 Corinthians 13, 13
Matthew 11, 28-30
2 Timothy 4, 6-8
James 5, 11
Luke 24, 50-end
Luke 18, 9-14
Song of Solomon 2, 3
1 Corinthians 1, 30
John 3, 7
John 13, 34-35
Song of Solomon 2, 3
Acts 11, 26
Isaiah 38, 1–
Song of Solomon 2, 3
Mark 4, 11–
Luke 19, 8-10
Psalm 24, 1–
Hebrews 7, 19–
Exodus 20, 1-7
Exodus 20, 8-11
Exodus 20, 12-13
Matthew 8, 1-4
Mark 9, 2-9
Psalm 119, 94
Exodus 20, 14-16
Psalm 107, 43
Exodus 20, 17
James 5, 14
Daniel 4, 30-33
Matthew 25, 31-33
Daniel 4, 34-37
Luke 8, 43-49
Isaiah 1, 10-19
Psalm 22, 27
Hebrews 11, 6
1 Peter 5, 8
Luke 22, 31-32
Hebrews 13, 1-3
Deuteronomy 10, 19
1 Timothy 4, 8
2 Corinthians 13, 13
1 Peter 5, 8
1 Peter 6, 8
Matthew 4, 1-8
Hebrews 8, 10-12
Hebrews 4, 16
Luke 10, 30-38
James 4, 14
Isaiah 57, 15

C. Published Works of Rev. Dr. James Muir

A Funeral Sermon in Memory of Captain Nathaniel Darrel [*of Christ Church, Warwick, Bermuda*]. St. George, Bermuda: Printed by Joseph Stockdale, King's Printer in Bermuda, n.d. (ca.1784-88). 18 p.

Sermons, by James Muir, A.M., Minister of the Presbyterian Church, Bermuda. Princeton, NJ: Printed by James Tod, 1787. 164 pages. Contents—Preface by John Witherspoon, I. A Profession of Christianity Universally Binding, II. The Necessity of Entering in at the Strait Gate (part 1), III. The Necessity of Entering in at the Strait Gate (part 2), IV. The Rich Man and Lazarus on Earth, V. The Rich Man and Lazarus in a Separate State, VI. Communicating the Duty of Every Christian, VII. Universal Benevolence Recommended, VIII. The Parable of the Rich Glutton (part 1), IX. The Parable of the Rich Glutton (part 2), X. The Parable of the Talents, XI. The Parable of the Talents (part 2), XII. The Parable of the Barren Fig-Tree (part 1), XIII. The Parable of the Barren Fig-Tree (part 2), XIV. Christ our Wisdom, Righteousness, Sanctification, and Redemption, XV. On Self Denial, XVI. The Freedom of the Gospel Call.

Comments at the Fixing of the First Boundary Stone for District of Columbia at Jones Point, April 15, 1791. *Virginia Gazette and Alexandria Advertiser*, 21 April 1791. Republished in *United States Gazette* (Philadelphia) April 30, 1791; *New-York Daily Gazette* 29 April 1791, page 2; *New York Magazine; or, Literary Repository* (New York City) 2 (May 1791): 301; *The Daily Advertiser* (New York City) 29 April 1791, page 2; *Connecticut Gazette* 12 May 1791 page 2; *Connecticut Courant* (Hartford) 9 May 1791, page 2; *City Gazette and Daily Advertiser* (Charleston, South Carolina); and elsewhere.

Extract of a letter from the Reverend Mr. James Muir, Principal of the Academy of Alexandria in Virginia, to the Author [Benjamin Rush of Philadelphia], dated July 29, 1791. In *The American Museum; or, Universal Magazine* 10 (August 1791): 61-63. Reprinted as Observations Upon the Study of the Latin and Greek Languages, as a Branch of Liberal Education, with Hints of a Plan of Liberal Instruction, without Them, Accommodated to the Present State of Society, Manners and Government in the United States. In Rush, Benjamin. *Essays, Literary, Moral & Philosophical*. Philadelphia: Printed by Thomas and Samuel F. Bradford, 1798. Pages 50-56.

The Virtuous Woman. In Austin, David. ed. *The American Preacher; or, a Collection of Sermons from Some of the Most Eminent Preachers, Now Living in the United States, of Different Denominations of the Christian Church; Never Before Published*. Four volumes. Elizabeth-town, NJ: Printed by Shepherd Kollock, 1791-93. In two parts, Sermon XXVII, Vol. II, pp. 145-157; Sermon XXVIII, Vol. II, pp. 159-170.

A Funeral Sermon [on Zechariah 1 5, in Memory of the Rev. James Hunt, Pastor of the Presbyterian congregations at Bladensburg and Cabin John, then known as Captain John, Maryland; and An Elegiac Poem by an anonymous author]. Alexandria, VA: Printed by Samuel Hanson and Thomas Bond, 1793. 20 pages.

A Pastoral Letter; to the Members of the Presbyterian Church Residing in Alexandria. Alexandria, VA: Printed by Samuel Hanson and Thomas Bond, 1793. 8 pages.

Proposals for Printing by Subscription an Examination of the Principles Contained in "The Age of Reason" in Ten Sermons, by James Muir, D.D., Minister of the Presbyterian Church, Alexandria. Alexandria, VA: Printer unknown, 1794. 1 page.

History of the Presbyterian Church at Alexandria from Its Formation A.D. 1772 Until Its Present State A.D. 1794. Unpublished two-page manuscript prepared in 1794, today held by the Presbyterian Historical Society, Philadelphia.

An Examination of the Principles Contained in [Thomas Paine's] "The Age of Reason;" in Ten Discourses. Baltimore, MD: Printed by Samuel and John Adams for the author. Sold by Ambrose Clarke and James Keddie, booksellers in Market Street, 1795. 166 pages. Contents—I. The Subject Introduced, II. The Nature of Inspiration Stated, III. Inspiration Argued from the Scriptures Themselves, IV. Inspiration Argued from Prophecy, V. Inspiration Argued from Miracles, VI. The Miracles Attending our Saviour's Death Considered, VII. The Scripture, an Ancient and Genuine Production, VIII. The Use of Reason in Religion, IX. A Moral Life Disposeth a Man to Receive, But an Immoral, to Reject the Gospel, X. America Warned, Delivered on Wednesday, 24th October 1793, Being a Fast-day Appointed by the Synod of Philadelphia.

Letter to Our Brethren, Members of the Presbyterian Church, Under the Care of the Transylvania Presbytery [Kentucky from the General Assembly of the Presbyterian Church in the U.S.A. Meeting in Carlisle, Pennsylvania in 1795]. (with Rev. David Rice and Elder Robert Patterson). In Presbyterian Church in the U.S.A. *Minutes of the General Assembly of the Presbyterian Church in the United States of America from its Organization A.D. 1789 to A.D. 1820 Inclusive.* Philadelphia: Presbyterian Board of Publication, 1847. Pp. 103-105.

A Sermon Preached in the Presbyterian Church at Alexandria on the 9th of May, 1798, Being the Day Appointed for a General Fast. Philadelphia: Printed by William Cobbett, 1798. 14 pages.

Pastoral Letter to the Churches [from the General Assembly Meeting in Winchester, Virginia in 1799]. (with Rev. Dr. John McKnight and Elder Jonathan Elmer). In Presbyterian Church in the U.S.A. *Minutes of the General Assembly of the Presbyterian Church in the United States of America from its Organization A.D. 1789 to A.D. 1820 Inclusive.* Philadelphia: Presbyterian Board of Publication, 1847. Pp. 177-179.

Funeral Sermon on the Death of General Washington, Delivered on the 29th ult. [December 1799] by the Revd. Dr. Muir. In *The Columbian Mirror and Alexandria Gazette*, 4 January 1800.

Dissertation, Delivered by the Rev. James Muir, on Saturday Last, [22 February 1800, the National Day of Mourning,] Prefatory to Doctor Dick's Eulogy on Gen. Washington, on the Respective Modes Pursued by Different Nations, at Different Periods, for Perpetuating the Memory of Deceased Personages of Eminence. In *The Columbian Mirror and Alexandria Gazette*, 27 February 1800. Reprinted in McGroarty, William Buckner. ed. *Washington: First in the Hearts of His Countrymen; the Orations by Men Who Had Known Washington in Person and Who Thus Could Speak with Authority.* Richmond, VA: Garrett and Massie, 1932. Pp. 47-53.

The Power of Godliness: Exemplified in the Remarkable Conversion and Triumphant Death of Mrs. Mary Davis of Bermuda. Alexandria, DC: Printed by J. and J. D. Westcott, 1802. 20 pages.

Instruction from the Grave: In Which are Unfolded the Behaviour, Sentiments, and Prospects of Persons of Different Ranks, Characters, and Stations, in Their Dying Moments; Given in Consequence of the Death of Oliver Deming Welman, who Died in the 21st Year of His Life, at Bermuda, on the 26th August, 1802. Alexandria, DC: Printed by John Westcott, 1803. 20 pages.

Death Abolished, a Sermon Occasioned by the Sickness Which Prevailed at Alexandria During the Months of August, September, and October [1803]: Giving a Detail of That Sickness, and of Some of the Views of Providence in Such Calamitous Visitations; with an Appendix, Containing Facts, Relating to the Origin of the Sickness, the Extent of the Mortality, the Labors of the Committee of Health, and the Contributions for the Relief of the Poor. Alexandria, DC: Printed by Cottom and Stewart, 1803; Alexandria, DC: Printed by Samuel Snowden for Robert and John Gray, 1814. 23 pages.

History of the Presbytery of Baltimore [from 1786 to 1804]. Original six-page manuscript prepared in 1804 is today held by the Presbyterian Historical Society, Philadelphia. Published as The History of the Presbytery of Baltimore in *Journal of Presbyterian History* 7 (June 1913): 105-109.

Of Nebuchadnezzar [Nebuchadnezzar II, the Babylonian king who Conquered Aram and Judah; Book of Daniel]. ("Philologos" – Lover of the Word – is used by Rev. Muir as his pseudonym). Issued in four parts; the first two parts are titled Of Nebuchadnezzar; the third part, Of Nebuchadnezzar, When Under Conviction; and the final part, Nebuchadnezzar, A Trophy of the Divine Grace. In *General Assembly's Missionary Magazine; or, Evangelical Intelligencer* 1 (August 1805): 375-378, 1 (September 1805): 421-424, 1 (November 1805): 531-534, and 1 (December 1805): 564-568.

The Decalogue [Ten Commandments]. (signed "Philologos" Lover of The Word). Issued in eleven parts; the final part is titled, Practical Remarks on the Decalogue. In *Panoplist* 1 (December 1805): 297-299, 1 (January 1806): 341-342, 1 (February 1806): 387-388, 1 (April 1806): 486-490, 2 (July 1806): 71-73, 2 (September 1806): 163-165, 2 (January 1807): 369-370, 2 (February 1807): 412-414, 2 (March 1807): 467-469, 2 (April 1807): 516-518, and 2 (May 1807): 547-549.

Of Angels. (signed "Philologos" Lover of the Word). Issued in six parts; the final four parts are titled, Of Apostate Angels. In *General Assembly's Missionary Magazine; or, Evangelical Intelligencer* 2 (January 1806): 25-29, 2 (February 1806): 74-78, 2 (March 1806): 114-118, 2 (April 1806): 167-170, 2 (May 1806): 215-220, and 2 (June 1806): 274-276.

Of Enoch ["who walked with God, and he was not, for God took him." Genesis 5:24]. (signed "Philologos" Lover of the Word). Issued in four parts. In *General Assembly's Missionary Magazine; or, Evangelical Intelligencer* 2 (November 1806): 517-521, 2 (December 1806): 563-565, 3 (January 1807): 22-26, and 3 (February 1807): 61-64.

The Messiah's Reign: A Sermon Preached on the Fourth of July, Before the Washington Society, and Published at Their Request. *Alexandria, DC: Printed by Samuel Snowden, 1806. 12 pages. Republished in part in* Panoplist *2 (December 1806): 327-328.*

Obituary [of Joanna Craig, who died at Alexandria, 21 October 1806]. *General Assembly's Missionary Magazine; or, Evangelical Intelligencer* 2 (December 1806): 596-597.

To Children and Youth; an Extract. (signed "Philologos" Lover of the Word). In *The Evidence; or, Religious and Moral Gazette* 1 (31 January 1807): 17-19.

The Young Christian: An Instructive Narrative. Alexandria, VA: Printed by Samuel Snowden, 1807. 8 pages. Republished in *Panoplist and Missionary Magazine* 2 (December 1809): 310-317; and (2) *The Advisor; or, Vermont Evangelical Magazine* 2 (March 1810): 79-83.

Observations on the Importance of the Present Life, as Introductory to the Future, from the Funeral Sermon, Delivered in Memory of Mrs. Mary Patten. Alexandria, DC: Printed by Cottom and Stewart, 1808. 17 pages.

The Efficacy and Goodness of Providence: A Sermon Preached before the Washington Society on the 22d February 1809. Alexandria, DC: Printed by Samuel Snowden, 1809. 8 pages.

A Pastoral Letter from the Ministers, or Bishops, and Ruling Elders of the Presbytery of Baltimore to All Under Their Respective Charges; on Various Duties; But, Especially, on the Religious Education of Their Youth. Baltimore, MD: Printed by Warner and Hanna for the Presbytery of Baltimore, 1811. 24 pages.

Repentance, or Richmond in Tears. Sermon with appendix. Alexandria, DC: Printed by Cottom and Stewart, 1812. Republished in *Ten Sermons.*

Ten Sermons. Alexandria, DC: Printed by Cottom and Stewart, 1812. 359 pages. Contents—I. The Signs of the Times, Delivered at the Episcopal Church on the 29th December A.D. 1811, II. Repentance, or Richmond in Tears (fire in Richmond, Virginia theater), III. Felix Trembling, IV. God's Claim Upon the Young, V. Religion Recommended to Youth, From the Infirmities Attending Old Age, VI. The Operations of the Spirit, the Seal of Heaven to the Truth of Christianity, VII. A Covenant, Securing to Men Temporal and Spiritual Blessings, VIII. The Christian Character, X. On Irresolution, and Appendix.

The Mortal and Immortal State, a Sermon; This Sermon, Delivered at Alexandria, on the 5th of September, in Testimony of Great Respect for the Memory of John Dundas, Esq., a Native of Philadelphia: Who Died on the 30th of August 1813, in the 55th Year of His Age, is Offered to Surviving Friends with Sympathy from the Author. Alexandria, DC: Printed by Samuel Snowden and John Douglass Simms, 1814. 11 pages.

An Address Prepared at the Desire of the Bible Society of the District of Columbia, at Their First Meeting, at Washington, on the 17th of April, 1814. New York: Published by Griffin and Rudd and Van Winkle and Wiley, 1814. 22 pages.

The True Patriot: A Sermon. Presented at the Request of the Washington Society of Alexandria, and Delivered Before Them at Christ's Church on the Fourth of July, 1814. In *Alexandria Gazette, Commercial & Political,* 16 July 1814.

Thanksgiving for Peace: A Sermon, Delivered in Christ's Church [Alexandria], on [a Day for Thanksgiving for the Restoration of Peace,] Thursday the 16th April. Alexandria, DC: Printed by Samuel Snowden, 1815.

Editor. *The Monthly Visitant; or, Something Old.* Alexandria, DC: Printed by Samuel Snowden. Issued July 1816, August 1816, September 1816, October 1816, November 1816, and December 1816. 240 pages.

The Call: A Sermon, Preached before the Presbytery of Baltimore at the Ordination of the Rev. Thomas B. Balch, in Georgetown, D.C. on Thursday 11th December, 1817... with an Appendix by the Rev. James Canahan, Detailing the Proceedings on That

Occasion. Georgetown, DC: Printed by W. A. Hind and Co., 1818. 26 pages. Extract as Considerations on a Call to the Ministry; Extract from an Ordination Sermon [Delivered at the Ordination of Rev. Thomas B. Balch, at Bridge-Street (Georgetown) Presbyterian Church, 11 December 1817]. *The Christian Messenger* 2 (11 April 1818): 353-355.

Register of Baptisms, Marriages, and Funerals during the Ministry of the Revd. Doctr. James Muir in the Presbyterian Church of Alexandria, D.C. [1789-1816]. Transcription of funeral information and portions of baptism and marriage information appears in Pippenger, Wesley E. *Tombstone Inscriptions of Alexandria Virginia*. Vol. 1. Westminster, MD: Family Line Publications, 1993. Transcription of marriage information appears in Pippenger, Wesley E. *Husbands and Wives Associated with Early Alexandria, Virginia (and the Surrounding Area)*. Third edition. Westminster, MD: Willow Bend Books, 2001.

D. Alexandria's Old Presbyterian Meeting House

The Presbyterians of Alexandria, present from the town's creation in 1749, initially worshiped with each other in reading houses (private homes) and at the Church of England, Virginia's established denomination until it is disestablishment in 1786. Beginning in 1760, they worshipped at formally organized services conducted in the Assembly Hall on Market Square, an eighteenth-century community-center type of facility that included a classroom, which served as the town's earliest school, and a public meeting room, which served as the meeting chamber of the town's Common Council, space for worship services, etc.

A formal congregation was established in 1772 when the Rev. William Thom (1750-1773) was called to serve as Alexandria's first installed Presbyterian minister. Thom, a native of Pennsylvania and graduate of the University of Pennsylvania, trained for the ministry under the Rev. Dr. John Witherspoon, President of the College of New Jersey (Princeton University). He was followed in the pulpit by the Rev. Dr. Isaac Stockton Keith (1755-1813) in 1780, a native of New Jersey who also graduated from the College of New Jersey and trained for the ministry under the Rev. Dr. Robert Smith at Pequea, Pennsylvania. The Rev. Dr. James Muir followed Keith in 1789.

During Rev. Muir's thirty-one year ministry, which encompassed the new nation's formative post-Revolutionary period, the congregation engaged in several specific acts and events that maintain prominent niches in Alexandria's collective memory. George Washington attended numerous charity sermons delivered at the Meeting House and at least one event with strong political overtones. In May 1798, while the nation contemplated the possibility of moving beyond its quasi-war with France to formal engagement, Washington attended the service led by the Rev. Muir for the National Day of Solemn Humiliation, Fasting, and Prayer (Muir 1798, Dickson 1987). In December 1799, when the beloved Washington died, the bell of the Meeting House, the town's only bell, tolled for the four days between his death and burial. Alexandria conducted four public memorial services, led by Rev. Muir and other local clergy, at the Meeting House (Muir 1800, McGroarty 1932, Kahler 2008).

In 1809, the congregation established Alexandria's Presbyterian Cemetery in response to a change in local laws that restricted new burials within city limits. In late 1811, the Meeting House was so shaken by the New Madrid, Missouri earthquake that its church bell rang (Muir 1812 pp. 18-20). In 1816, the congregation supported publication of a religious journal, *The Monthly Visitant; or, Something Old*, founded and edited by Rev. Muir (Muir 1816), and established a Sabbath Day school that was conducted by lay teachers and elders (Boylan 1988). Hymn singing was introduced into worship services during the 1790s, which after 1817 was supported by a pipe organ built by Jacob Hilbus of Washington, D.C. It is the earliest known instance of an American Presbyterian congregation installing a pipe organ in their place of worship (Melton 1967).

When Alexandria's second Presbyterian congregation was established in 1817, the congregation at the Meeting House, which until then had been known simply as the Presbyterian Church, took First Presbyterian Church as its new name. The scholarly Rev. Dr. Elias Harrison (1790-1863), who had served as Rev. Muir's co-pastor for three years, succeeded him as the congregation's sole minister when Muir died in 1820. Harrison led the congregation through his death in the midst of the Civil War in 1863. An open advocate for the elimination of slavery and the administration of free public education, Harrison once referred to the pre-war years as a time of "sore domestic trials," and just prior to his death, spoke wearily of going "where the storm cloud of war can never hover."

The Meeting House remained open for worship throughout the Civil War and remained part of the Presbyterian Church in the U.S.A., while Second Presbyterian joined the newly formed Presbyterian Church in the U.S. A few years after the war, large portions of Alexandria's two Presbyterian congregations joined together to form the Union Presbyterian Church, "looking for a union of the whole Presbyterian family North and South." Led by the Rev. Dr. J. J. Bullock (1812-1892), who also served as Chaplain of the U.S. Senate, the experiment in unity lasted from 1874 into 1880. At the close of the nineteenth century and while still part of the Presbyterian Church in the U.S.A., the congregation was unable to call a minister willing to serve here. Still active and with seventy-two communicant members on entering the final decade of the century, but with no installed minister, the congregation was formally dissolved in 1899.

For the next half-century the Meeting House facilities were utilized by Second Presbyterian Church, which itself would dissolve in 2002. In 1949, a formal congregation was once again established at the Meeting House as part of the Presbyterian Church in the U.S. It has thrived since then as the Old Presbyterian Meeting House and is now a congregation of 1,000 members in a reunited Presbyterian Church U.S.A.

The original Meeting House structure, the one known by the Rev. Dr. Muir, was erected in 1775 in the 300-block of South Fairfax Street. It was struck by lightning and largely destroyed in 1835. When rebuilt, it again utilized the plain-style architectural tradition that is sometimes referred to as the meeting-house style and is long associated with Reformed Protestant denominations in America (Bruggink and Droppers 1965, Buggeln 1999, Williams 1999). The rebuilt Meeting House, with its original plain-style architecture remarkably well-preserved, continues to serve the congregation today (Figure 3).

The Meeting House is located in what is popularly known as Old Town Alexandria, an area recognized by the U.S. Department of the Interior as a National Historic Landmark District that retains much of the character that existed when George Washington and the Rev. Muir walked its streets (Moore 1949, Smith and Miller 1989, Madison 2003). The Meeting House structure is recognized by the U.S. Department of the Interior as a National Historic Place; by the Commonwealth of Virginia as a Historic Landmark; and by the Presbyterian Historical Society as a site that is important in the history of Presbyterian and Reformed denominations in the United States. The Meeting House and its adjoining Elliot House are also recognized locally by the Historic Alexandria Foundation as structures that have maintained their historic and architectural integrity. Both structures were also included in the Historic American Buildings Survey, which was conducted during the 1930s by the U.S. Department of the Interior. The churchyard Burial Ground, with its Tomb of the Unknown Soldier of the American Revolution, and the congregation's Presbyterian Cemetery contain the graves of nearly fifty Revolutionary War patriots. Both are both included in the Sons of the American Revolution's National Register of the American Revolution.

Figure 3. The Old Presbyterian Meeting House at Alexandria, Virginia Today. (Drawing by Betty Heiby, 1974)

Bibliography

Achenbach, Joel. 2004. *The Grand Idea: George Washington's Potomac and the Race to the West.* New York: Simon and Schuster.

Ahlstrom, Sydney E. 1972. *A Religious History of the American People.* New Haven, CT: Yale University Press.

Alexandria Association. 1956. *Our Town: 1749-1865; Likenesses of This Place & Its People Taken from Life, by Artists Known and Unknown.* Alexandria, VA: Alexandria Association.

Allen, Gloria Seaman. 2001. Needlework Education in Ante-bellum Alexandria, Virginia. *The Magazine Antiques* (February): 332-341.

Allen, Gloria Seaman. 1996-97. Equally Their Due: Female Education in Antebellum Alexandria. *Historic Alexandria Quarterly* 1 (Summer): 1-11; 1 (Late Summer): 1-13; and 1 (Winter): 1-15.

Ambrose, Stephen E. 1996. *Undaunted Courage: Meriwether Lewis, Thomas Jefferson, and the Opening of the American West.* New York: Simon and Schuster.

Anderberg, Lorna and John G. Motheral. 1996. *A Comparison of Alexandria Quakers to the Population of White Alexandria.* Alexandria Archaeology Publications No. 28. Alexandria, VA: Alexandria Archaeology, Office of Historic Alexandria, City of Alexandria.

Anderson, Ellen. 1979. *Salona: Fairfax County, Virginia.* Fairfax, VA: Fairfax County Office of Comprehensive Planning.

Asbury, Francis. 1821. *The Journal of Francis Asbury, Bishop of the Methodist Church, August 7, 1771 - December 7, 1815.* Three volumes. New York: N. Bangs and T. Mason.

Bercovitch, Sacvan. 1978. *The American Jeremiad.* Madison, WI: University of Wisconsin Press.

Boles, John B. 1972. *The Great Revival, 1787-1805: The Origins of the Southern Evangelical Mind.* Lexington, KY: University Press of Kentucky.

Boller, Jr. Paul F. 1961. George Washington and the Presbyterians. *Journal of the Presbyterian Historical Society* [*Journal of Presbyterian History*] 39 (September): 129-149.

Boylan, Anne M. 1988. *The Sunday School: The Formation of an American Institution, 1790-1880.* New Haven, CT: Yale University Press.

Brockett, Franklin L. and Alfred G. Uhler. 1899 (1876). *The Lodge of Washington: A History of the Alexandria-Washington Lodge No. 22, A. F. and A. M. of Alexandria, Va. 1783-1876; Compiled from the Original Records of the Lodge... Together with an Appendix Bringing the*

Record Down to the Close of Nineteenth Century. Alexandria, VA: Published by G. H. Ramey and Son for the Alexandria-Washington Lodge.

Bromberg, Francine W. et al. 1999. *A Community Digs Its Past: The Lee Street Site*. Alexandria, VA: Alexandria Archaeology, Office of Historic Alexandria, City of Alexandria.

Bromberg, Francine W. and Steven J. Shepard. 2006. The Quaker Burying Ground in Alexandria, Virginia: A Study of Burial Practices of the Religious Society of Friends. *Historical Archaeology* 40: 57-88.

Brown, Ralph H. 1943. *Mirror for Americans: Likeness of the Eastern Seaboard, 1810*. Special Publication No. 27. New York: American Geographical Society.

Bruce, Jr., Dickson D. 1974. *And They All Sang Hallelujah: Plain-Folk Camp-Meeting Religion, 1800-1845*. Knoxville, TN: University of Tennessee Press.

Bruggink, Donald J. and Carl H. Droppers. 1965. *Christ and Architecture: Building Presbyterian/Reformed Churches*. Grand Rapids, MI: William B. Eerdmans.

Brumbaugh, Gaius M. 1918-20. Marriage Licenses of the District of Columbia. *National Genealogical Society Quarterly* 7 (October 1918): 33-39, 7 (January 1919): 49-53, 8 (April-July 1919): 27-31, 8 (January 1920): 55-57.

Buggeln, Gretchen Townsend. 1999. Elegance and Sensibility in the Calvinist Tradition: The First Congregational Church of Hartford, Connecticut. In Finney, Paul Corby. ed. *Seeing Beyond the Word: Visual Arts and the Calvinist Tradition*. Grand Rapids, MI: William B. Eerdmans. Pp. 429-455.

Burrows, Edwina G. and Mike Wallace. 1999. *Gotham: A History of New York City to 1898*. New York: Oxford University Press.

Caldwell, John Edwards. 1951 (1810). *A Tour through Part of Virginia, in the Summer of 1808; Also, Some Account of the Islands in the Atlantic Ocean, Known by the Name of the Azores, Visited for Some Weeks by the Author, on His way From the Untied States to Europe, in April and May, 1809*. Reprint of the 1810 Belfast edition, with editing by William M. E. Rachel. Richmond, VA: Dietz Press.

Cranch, William. 1812. *Report of Cases Argued and Adjudged in the Supreme Court of the United States, in February Term 1805 and February Term 1806*. Second edition. New York: C. Wiley.

Cresswell, Nicholas. 1924. *The Journal of Nicholas Cresswell*. Edited by Lincoln Macveagh. New York: Dial Press.

Cross, Whitney R. 1950. *The Burned-Over District: The Social and Intellectual History of Enthusiastic Religion in Western New York, 1800-1850*. Ithaca, NY: Cornell University Press.

Crothers, A. Glenn. 2001. Agricultural Improvement and Technological Innovation in a Slave Society: The Case of Early National Northern Virginia. *Agricultural History* 75: 135-169.

Cox, Ethelyn. 1976. *Historic Alexandria Virginia Street by Street: A Survey of Existing Early Buildings*. McLean, VA: EPM Publications for Historic Alexandria Foundation.

Davis, Deering, Stephen P. Dorsey, Ralph Cole Hall, and Nancy McClelland. 1946. *Alexandria Houses 1750-1830*. New York: Architectural Book Publishing Co.

Davis, Susan G. 1986. *Parades and Power: Street Theatre in Nineteenth-Century Philadelphia*. Philadelphia, Temple University Press.

Dickson, Charles Ellis. 1987. Jeremiads in the New American Republic: The Case of National Fasts in the John Adams Administration. *New England Quarterly* 60 (June): 187-207.

Dow, Richard B. 1952. *A History of the Second Presbyterian Church, Alexandria, Virginia 1817-1950*. Richmond, VA: Privately printed by Garrett & Massie for Second Presbyterian Church.

Duncan, John M. 1823. *Travels Through Part of the United States and Canada in 1818 and 1819*. Two volumes. Glasgow, Scotland: Glasgow University Press.

Eaves, Robert Wendell. 1936. A History of the Educational Developments of Alexandria, Virginia, Prior to 1860. *William and Mary Quarterly* Second series, 16 (April): 111-161.

Fletcher, W. Fred. 2003. *Light on the Hill: Bicentennial History of First Baptist Church, Alexandria, Virginia*. Alexandria, VA: Privately printed for First Baptist Church.

Gamble, Robert S. 1973. *Sully: The Biography of a House*. Chantilly, VA: Sully Foundation.

Gaustad, Edwin S. and Mark A. Noll. eds. 2003 (1982). *A Documentary History of Religion in America*. Two volumes. Grand Rapids, MI: William B. Eerdmans Publishing Co. (Plan of Union: Congregationalists and Presbyterians, Vol. I, pp. 371-375.)

General Association of Connecticut. 1805. *Extracts from the Minutes of the General Association of Connecticut, Holden at Guilford, A.D. 1805*. Hartford, CT: Hudson and Goodwin.

Glazier, Stephen D. 2005. Camp Meeting Grounds. In Feintuch, Burt and David H. Watters. eds. *The Encyclopedia of New England: The Culture and History of an American Region*. New Haven, CT: Yale University Press. P. 1297.

Guy, Kitty, *et al*. 1995. *St. Mary's [Roman Catholic Church]: 200 Years for Christ, 1795-1995*. Alexandria, VA: Privately printed for St. Mary's Roman Catholic Church.

Hambleton, Elizabeth and Marian Van Landingham. eds. 1975. *Alexandria: A Composite History*. Alexandria, VA: Alexandria Bicentennial Commission.

Hedman, Kathryn Pierpoint. ed. 1974. *Washington Street United Methodist Church, Alexandria, Virginia: Reflections 1849-1974*. Alexandria, VA: Privately printed for Washington Street United Methodist Church.

Heinemann, Ronald L., John G. Kolp, Anthony S. Parent Jr., and William G. Shade. 2007. *Old Dominion, New Commonwealth: A History of Virginia, 1607-2007*. Charlottesville, VA: University of Virginia Press.

Henry, James R. 1977. Churches. In Macoll, John D. and George J. Stansfield. eds. *Alexandria: A Towne in Transition, 1800-1900*. Alexandria, VA: Alexandria Bicentennial Commission and Alexandria Historical Society. Pp. 124-142.

Herrick, Carole L. 2005. *August 24, 1814: Washington in Flames*. Falls Church, VA: Higher Education Publications, Inc.

Hurst, Harold W. 1991. *Alexandria on the Potomac: The Portrait of an Antebellum Community*. Lanham, MD: University Press of America.

Isaac, Rhys. 1982. *The Transformation of Virginia, 1740-1790*. Chapel Hill, NC: University of North Carolina Press for the Institute of Early American History and Culture of Williamsburg, Virginia.

Janson, Charles William. 1807. *The Stranger in America: Containing Observations Made During a Long Residence in that Country, on the Genius, Manners and Customs of the People of the United States; with Biographical Particulars of Public Characters; Hints and Facts Relative to the Arts, Science, Commerce, Agriculture, Manufactures, Emigration, and the Slave Trade... Illustrated by Engravings*. London: Printed for J. Cundee.

Kabler, Dorothy Holcombe. 1957. Early Cabinet Makers. *Yearbook of the Alexandria Association*. Printed by Newell-Cole Co. for the Association. Pp. 65-75.

Kahler, Gerald E. 2008. *The Long Farewell: Americans Mourn the Death of George Washington*. Charlottesville, VA: University of Virginia Press.

Kennedy, Jean deChantal. 1964. *Frith of Bermuda, a Gentleman Privateer: A Biography of Hezekiah Frith, 1763-1848*. Hamilton, Bermuda: Bermuda Press.

Laha, Jr., Robert R. 2002. *Jeremiah*. Interpretation Bible Studies series. Louisville, KY: Westminster John Knox Press.

Lambert, Frank. 2005. *The Barbary Wars: American Independence in the Atlantic World*. New York: Hill and Wang.

Larkin, Jack. 1988. *The Reshaping of Everyday Life, 1790-1840*. New York: Harper and Row.

Larkin, Jack. 2006. *Where We Lived: Discovering the Places We Once Called Home; The American Home from 1775 to 1840.* Newtown, CT: Taunton Press.

Lee, Edmund Jennings. 1895. *Lee of Virginia, 1642-1892: Biographical and Genealogical Sketches of the Descendents of Colonel Richard Lee.* Philadelphia: Franklin Printing Co.

Lloyd House Staff. 1997. *Obituary Notices from the Alexandria Gazette, 1784-1915 (Revised).* Lovettsville, VA: Willow Bend Books.

Mackay, James C. 2000. The Development of Early Taverns in Alexandria. *Historic Alexandria Quarterly* 5: 1-10.

Macoll, John D. ed. 1977. *Alexandria: A Towne in Transition, 1800-1900.* Alexandria, VA: Alexandria Bicentennial Commission and Alexandria Historical Society.

Madison, Robert L. 2003. *Walking with Washington: Walking Tours of Alexandria Virginia, Featuring Over 100 Sites Associated with George Washington.* Baltimore, MD: Gateway Press.

Massie, Henry. 1922 (1808). Journal of Captain Henry Massie [Kept Between Fredericksburg in Virginia and Boston in Massachusetts, April, May and June 1808]. *Tyler's Quarterly Historical and Genealogical Magazine* 4 (October): 77-86.

McCarty, Clara S. 1976. *Duels in Virginia and Nearby Bladensburg.* Richmond, Virginia: Dietz Press.

McGroarty, William B. 1928. The Washington Society of Alexandria. *Tyler's Quarterly Historical and Genealogical Magazine* 9 (January): 147-163.

McGroarty, William B. ed. 1932. *Washington: First in the Hearts of His Countrymen—the Orations by Men Who Had Known Washington in Person and Who Thus Could Speak with Authority.* Richmond, VA: Garrett and Massie.

McGroarty, William B. 1940a. *The Old Presbyterian Meeting House at Alexandria, Virginia 1774-1874.* Richmond, VA: Privately printed by William Byrd Press.

McGroarty, William B. 1940b. Reverend James Muir, D.D., and Washington's Orphan Wards. *William and Mary Quarterly* Second series, 20 (October): 511-523.

McGroarty, William B. 1940c. Alexandria Academy. *William and Mary Quarterly* Second series, 20 (April): 253-260.

McGroarty, William B. 1941. Alexandria's Lancasterian Schools. *William and Mary Quarterly* Second series, 30 (April): 111-118.

McKenney, Ashton N. 1958. *A History of the Relief Truck and Engine Company No. 1 of the Alexandria Fire Department Alexandria, Virginia.* Alexandria, VA: Privately printed.

McKim, Randolph H. 1894. *Washington's Church: An Historical Sketch of Old Christ Church*, Alexandria, Virginia, *Together with a Brief Description of the Centenary Services Therein, November 20 and 21st 1873*. Alexandria, VA: Privately printed by Robert Bell's Sons, Stationers and Printers for the Ladies Sewing Guild of Christ (Episcopal) Church.

Melton, Julius. 1967. *Presbyterian Worship in America: Changing Patterns since 1787*. Richmond, VA: John Knox Press.

Miller, T. Michael. 1987. *Alexandria & Alexandria (Arlington) County, Virginia Minister Returns & Marriage Bonds, 1801-1852*. Bowie, MD: Heritage Books.

Miller, T. Michael. ed. 1987. *Pen Portraits of Alexandria, Virginia 1739-1900*. Bowie, MD: Heritage Books.

Miller, T. Michael. ed. 1988. *Murder & Mayhem: Criminal Conduct in Old Alexandria, Virginia, 1749-1900*. Bowie, MD: Heritage Books.

Miller, T. Michael. 1991-92. *Artisans and Merchants of Alexandria, Virginia, 1780-1820*. Two volumes. Bowie, MD: Heritage Books.

Miller, T. Michael. 1992. Weathering the Storm. *The Fireside Sentinel* 6 (March): 13-24.

Minter-Dowd, Christine. 1979. *Made in Alexandria: An Exhibit of Decorative Arts*. Alexandria, VA: Alexandria Bicentennial Commission and the Rotary Club of Alexandria.

Morgan, Jr., Henry G. 1977. Education. In Macoll, John D. ed. *Alexandria: A Towne in Transition 1800-1900*. Alexandria, VA: Alexandria Bicentennial Commission and Alexandria Historical Society. Pp. 89-123.

Morrill, Penny C. 1987. Alexandria Academy: The Birth of Universal Education in America. *The Plaque: A Publication of the Historic Alexandria Foundation* 2 (Autumn): 10-15.

Morrison, Ellen Earnhardt. 1979. *The Church That Keeps Memories Alive: The Story of Christ Church, Alexandria, Virginia*. Alexandria, VA: Privately printed for Christ (Episcopal) Church.

Moore, Gay Montague. 1949. *Seaport in Virginia: George Washington's Alexandria*. Richmond, VA: Garrett and Massie.

Mosheim, Johann Lorenz. 1797-98. *An Ecclesiastical History: Antient and Modern, From the Birth of Christ, to the Beginning of the Present Century; In Which the Rise, Progress, and Variations of Church Power are Considered in their Connexion with the State of Learning and Philosophy, and the Political History of Europe During That Period, by the Late Learned John Lawrence Mosheim; Translated from the Original Latin, and Accompanied with Notes and Chronological Tables by Archibald Maclaine, D.D.* Six volumes. First American edition. Philadelphia: Printed by Stephen C. Ustick.

Moulton, Gary E. ed. *The Journals of the Lewis and Clark Expedition*. Thirteen volumes plus atlas. Lincoln, NB: University of Nebraska Press, 1983-2001.

Muir, Rev. James. various dates. Copies of the cited letters exchanged by Rev. Muir with others are held by the Meeting House Archive.

Munson, James D. 1990-91. *Alexandria, Virginia Hustings Court Deeds, 1783-1797* and *Alexandria Virginia Hustings Court Deeds, 1797-1801*. Bowie, MD: Heritage Books.

Nash, Gary B. 1965. The American Clergy and the French Revolution. *William and Mary Quarterly* Third series, 22 (July): 392-412.

Nelson, John K. 2001. *A Blessed Company: Parishes, Parsons, and Parishioners in Anglican Virginia, 1690-1776*. Chapel Hill: University of North Carolina Press.

Netherton, Nan, Donald Sweig, Janice Artemel, Patricia Hicken, and Patrick Reed. 1978. *Fairfax County Virginia: A History*. Fairfax, VA: Fairfax County Board of Supervisors.

Noll, Mark. 1992. *A History of Christianity in the United States and Canada*. Grand Rapids, MI: W. B. Eerdmans.

Nord, David Paul. 2002. Benevolent Capital: Financing Evangelical Book Publishing in Early Nineteenth-Century America. In Noll, Mark. ed. *God and Mammon: Protestants, Money, and the Market, 1790-1860*. New York: Oxford University Press. Pp. 147-170.

Noricks, Ronald H. 1982. "Jealousies & Contentions": The Plan of Union and the Western Reserve, 1801-37. *Journal of Presbyterian History* 60 (Summer): 130-143.

Old Presbyterian Meeting House (Presbyterian Church at Alexandria). various dates. Unpublished records of the congregation include Registers of the congregation's communicant members, marriages, baptisms, and funerals, minutes of Session and Church Committee meetings, Sunday school rosters, etc. They are retained in the Meeting House Archive. A brief account of the congregation's history, biographical sketches of its clergy, and description of its churchyard and facilities are available at the congregation's website – www.opmh.org.

Olson, Sherry H. 1980. *Baltimore: The Building of an American City*. Baltimore, MD: Johns Hopkins University Press.

Peterson, Arthur G. 1932. The Alexandria Market Prior to the Civil War. *William and Mary Quarterly* Second series, 12 (April): 104-114.

Pippenger, Wesley E. 1991. *Husbands and Wives Associated with Early Alexandria, Virginia*. Westminster, MD: Family Line Publications.

Powell, Mary Gregory. 2000 (1928). *The History of Old Alexandria, Virginia from July 13, 1749 to May 24, 1861*. Westminster, MD: Willow Bend Books.

Presbyterian Church in the U.S.A. 1847. *Minutes of the General Assembly of the Presbyterian Church in the United States of America from Its Organization A.D. 1789 to A.D. 1820 Inclusive.* Philadelphia: Presbyterian Board of Publication.

Presbytery of Baltimore (Synod of Philadelphia, Presbyterian Church in the U.S.A.). Various dates. *Minutes.*

Rehnquist, William. 1992. *Grand Inquests: The Historic Impeachments of Samuel Chase and President Andrew Johnson.* New York: Morrow.

Reinhold, Meyer. 1968. Opponents of Classical Learning in America during the Revolutionary Period. *Proceedings of the American Philosophical Society* 112 (August): 221-234.

Riston, Mrs. Anne. 1809. *A Poetical Picture of America: Being Observations Made, During a Residence of Several Years at Alexandria, and Norfolk, in Virginia; Illustrating the Manners and Customs of the Inhabitants: And Interspersed with Anecdotes, Arising from a General Intercourse with Society in That Country, from the Year 1799 to 1807; by a Lady*. London: Printed for the author by W. Wilson.

Robbins, Thomas. 1886-87. *Diary of Thomas Robbins, D.D., 1796-1854...Edited and Annotated by Increase N. Tarbox.* Two volumes. Boston: Printed by Thomas Todd.

Robinson, Deborah. 2007-08. Taverns in Early Northern Virginia. *Yearbook: The Historical Society of Fairfax County, Virginia* 31: 1-36.

Seale, William. 2007. *The Alexandria Library Company.* New Castle, DE: Oak Knoll Books.

Sengel, William R. 1973. *Can These Bones Live? Pastoral Reflections on the Old Presbyterian Meeting House of Alexandria, Virginia Through Its First Two Hundred Years.* Kingsport, TN: Privately printed by Kingsport Press for the Old Presbyterian Meeting House.

Shomette, Donald G. 2003. *Maritime Alexandria: The Rise and Fall of an American Entrepôt.* Bowie, MD: Heritage Books.

Skarmeas, Nancy J. 2004. *The Ideals Guide to Historic Places of Worship in the United States.* Nashville, TN: Ideals Press.

Smith, Elwyn A. 1962. *The Presbyterian Ministry in American Culture: A Study in Changing Concepts 1700-1900.* Philadelphia: Westminster Press for Presbyterian Historical Society.

Smith, Joseph T. 1899. *Eighty Years: Embracing a History of Presbyterianism in Baltimore.* Philadelphia, PA: Westminster Press.

Smith, Peter J. C., William Robson Notman, Joseph H. S. Frith, Ernest A. McCallan, Esther K. Law, and Archibald N. Smith. 1984. *Presbyterians in Bermuda, 1609-1984: A Wholesome Leaven, The Story of Christ Church, Warwick, Bermuda; A Compilation of Six Narratives Dealing with Its History.* Bermuda: Printed by Engravers Limited for the Kirk Session of Christ Church.

Smith, William Francis and T. Michael Miller. 1989. *A Seaport Saga: Portrait of Old Alexandria, Virginia.* Virginia Beach, VA: Donning Company Publishers.

Smylie, James H. 1972-73. Classical Perspectives on Deism: Paine's "Age of Reason" in Virginia. *Eighteenth-Century Studies* 6 (Winter): 203-220.

Smylie, James H. 1985. *American Presbyterians: A Pictorial History.* Special issue of *Journal of Presbyterian History* 63, 1 and 2 (Spring and Summer 1985). Philadelphia: Presbyterian Historical Society.

Smylie, James H. 1996. *A Brief History of the Presbyterians.* Louisville, KY: Geneva Press.

Solberg, Winton U. 1977. The Chesapeake Colonies. In *Redeem the Time: The Puritan Sabbath in Early America.* Cambridge, MA: Harvard University Press. Pp. 85-106.

Sorin, Gretchen Sullivan. 1981. Tavern Fare Comestibles in Alexandria, 1770-1810. *Northern Virginia Heritage* 3 (November): 3-6, 14 and 20.

Sorin, Gretchen Sullivan. 1982. The Tavern in Northern Virginia Society. *Northern Virginia Heritage* 4 (June): 3-6 and 20.

Sprague, William B. *et al.* 1858. James Muir, D.D. In Sprague, William B. ed. *Annals of the American Pulpit: or, Commemorative Notices of Distinguished American Clergymen of Various Denominations....* Nine volumes (1857-69). Vol. 3, *Presbyterians*, pp. 516-521. New York: Robert Carter and Brothers.

Sprouse, Edith Moore. 2001. *Along the Potomac River: Extracts from the "Maryland Gazette," 1728-1799.* Westminster, MD: Willow Bend Books.

Stauffer, Vernon. 1918. *New England and the Bavarian Illuminati.* New York: Columbia University Press.

Sutcliff, Robert. 1811. *Travels in Some Parts of North America, in the Years 1804, 1805, & 1806.* York, England: Printed by C. Peacock for W. Alexander.

Sweet, William W. 1936. *Religion on the American Frontier, 1783-1840: A Collection of Documents; The Presbyterians.* Chicago: University of Chicago Press.

Stowell, Marion Barber. 1977. *Early American Almanacs: The Colonial Weekday Bible.* New York: Burt Franklin.

Stukenbroeker, Fern C. 1974. *A Watermelon for God: A History of Trinity United Methodist Church Alexandria, Virginia 1794-1974.* Alexandria, VA: Privately printed for Trinity United Methodist Church.

Thomas, Jr., Arthur Dicken. 1983. Reasonable Revivalism: Presbyterian Evangelization of Educated Virginias, 1787-1837. *Journal of Presbyterian History* 61 (Fall): 316-334.

Thompson, Ernest Trice. 1963. The Pastor and His People. In *Presbyterians in the South: 1607-1861* of *Presbyterians in the South*. Three volumes, 1963-73. Richmond, VA: John Knox Press. Vol. I, pp. 212-234.

Thompson, Ernest Trice. 1963-73. *Presbyterians in the South: 1607-1861* of *Presbyterians in the South*. Three volumes. Richmond, VA: John Knox Press.

Thompson, William E. 1989. *'A Set of Rebellious Scoundrels': Three Centuries of Presbyterians Along the Potomac*. Hampden Sydney, VA: Hampden-Sydney College Chapel.

Toll, Ian W. 2006. *Six Frigates: The Epic History of the Founding of the U.S. Navy*. New York: W. W. Norton and Co.

Van Horn, Hugh M. 2009. *The Presbyterian Cemetery, Alexandria, Virginia, 1809-2009*. Alexandria, VA: Privately printed by Arlington Press for Old Presbyterian Meeting House.

Vedeler, Harold C. 1996. *A History of the Old Presbyterian Meeting House*. Alexandria, VA: Old Presbyterian Meeting House.

Voges, Nettie Allen. 1977. Everyday Life. In Macoll, John D. and George J. Stansfield. eds. *Alexandria: A Towne in Transition, 1800-1900*. Alexandria, VA: Alexandria Bicentennial Commission and Alexandria Historical Society. Pp. 192-203.

Voges, Nettie Allen. 1975. *Old Alexandria: Where America's Past is Present*. McLean, VA: EPM Publications.

Wallace, Alton S. 2003. *I Once Was Young: History of the Alfred Street Baptist Church 1803-2003*. Alexandria, VA: Privately printed for Alfred Street Baptist Church.

Wardell, Patrick G. 1986. *Alexandria City and County Virginia Wills, Administrations and Guardian Bonds, 1800-1870*. Bowie, MD: Heritage Books.

Watson, Richard. 1791 (1785). *A Collection of Theological Tracts*. Six volumes. Second edition. London: T. Evans.

Watters, William. 1806. *A Short Account of the Christian Experience, and Ministerial Labours of William Watters; Drawn Up by Himself*. Alexandria, VA: Printed by Samuel Snowden.

Whitton, Robert G. 1982. The Washington Society of Alexandria. *Alexandria History* 4: 5-9.

Williams, Peter W. 1999. Metamorphoses of the Meetinghouse: Three Case Studies. In Finney, Paul Corby. ed. *Seeing Beyond the Word: Visual Arts and the Calvinist Tradition*. Grand Rapids, MI: William B. Eerdmans. Pp. 479-505.

Witham, Larry. 2007. *A City Upon a Hill: How Sermons Changed the Course of American History*. New York: HarperCollins Publishers.

Wosh, Peter J. 1994. *Spreading the Word: The Bible Business in Nineteenth-Century America*. Ithaca, NY: Cornell University Press.

Wright, F. Edward and Wesley E. Pippenger. 1996. *Early Church Records of Alexandria City and Fairfax County, Virginia*. Westminster, MD: Family Line Publications.

Index

Addison, Joseph, 67
Addison, Walter D., 63
African American (Negro), 3, 42
Alexandria Academy, 2, 13, 27, 30-31, 57, 59, 62, 66, 67, 79, 95
Alexandria Board of Guardians of the Free Schools, 13
Alexandria Library Company, 2, 12, 23, 24, 50, 67, 72, 78, 79, 91
Alexandria Society for the Promotion of Useful Knowledge, 12, 57
Ashford, George, 87

Balch, Rev. Stephen Bloomer, 23, 38, 42, 72, 74, 81
Baptismal services, 5, 7, 34, 41, 42, 44, 48-49, 60, 71, 101
Baptist Church (Alexandria), 5
Baltimore (Maryland), 3, 5, 7, 8, 27, 28, 29, 32, 37, 38, 39-41, 42, 43, 44, 45, 50, 51-52, 59, 70, 73, 74-75, 76-77, 92
Baxter, Rev. George A., 81-82
Bermuda, 2, 7, 8, 10, 12, 26, 40, 44-45, 46, 54, 57, 61, 69, 88, 90-91, 95, 97, 98
Bible, 14, 15, 22, 42, 93, *passim*.
  texts for sermons by Rev. Muir during 1805 listed, 93
Bible Society of the District of Columbia, 12, 16, 100
Black, David, 34
Black, Eliza, 34
Bogan, Elizabeth (Mrs. Frederick Shuck), 33
Boggs, Rev. John, 34-36
Bowie, John F., 37, 64-65
Bowling, George, 31
Brackenridge, Rev. John, 91-92
Brainerd, Rev. Israel, 55
Brick Presbyterian Church (New York City), 12, 52, 59
Bridge-Street Presbyterian Church, *See* Georgetown Presbyterian Church
Brockett, Robert 1

Broome, John, 53
Brothers, John Fair, 46
Burford, John Atkins, 63-64, 83-84
Burial Ground (at Old Presbyterian Meeting House), 25, 31, 60, 69, 83, 103-104
Burials, *See* funerals
Burr, Aaron, 8, 21-22, 37

Call, Polley (Mrs. Samuel Endicott), 74
Catholic, Roman, 5, 29
Cemetery, *See* Burial Ground
Chantilly Estate (Fairfax County, Virginia), 2, 7-8, 23, 24, 40, 45, 50-51, 60, 67-68, 83, 87
Chapin, Rev. Calvin, 55-56
Charleston (South Carolina), 3, 76, 77, 79-80, 82, 86
Chase, Justice Samuel, impeachment trial, 7, 27-29, 31-32
Christ Church, *See* Episcopal Church (Alexandria)
Christ (Church of Scotland) Church (Bermuda), 10, 54, 88, 94
Christian education, *See* Sabbath Day School
Clinton, George, 82
College of New Jersey (Princeton University), 10, 25, 27, 46, 59, 68, 72, 92, 102
Colross Estate (Alexandria), 37, 64
Columbian Academy (Georgetown, D.C.), 92
Communion, *See* Lord's Supper
Compton, Susana (Mrs. George Ashford), 87
Congregational Churches in Connecticut, General Association of, 45, 48, 49-50, 54-56, 91
Cottom, Peter, x, 17, 26, 98-100
Craig, Samuel, 21, 79, 90-91
Craig, Joanna, 21, 91, 99
Cresswell, Nicholas, 74

Davis, Josiah Hewes, 37-38
Davis, Mary (Bermuda), 97

Davis, Mary (Mrs. Henry Lyles), 77
Davis, Sarah M. (Mrs. Josiah), 34
Davis, Sarah (Mrs. John Harper), 51
Day, Rev. Jeremiah, 54
Deneale, George, 32
Dick, Elisha Cullen, 13, 30-31, 46, 51, 76
Dick, Julia (Mrs. Gideon Pearce), 76
Dixon, John, 41
Douglass, James, 78
Dueling, 6, 8, 21-22, 37-38, 53, 64-67
Dumfries (Prince William County, Virginia), 60
Dundas, Agnes (Mrs. John), 49, 71
Dundas, John, 48-49, 60, 100
Dunlop, Elizabeth (Mrs. John), 80
Dunlop, John, 79-80, 82
Dwight, Timothy, 8, 53

Edinburgh, University of (Scotland), 10, 24, 52, 86, 92
Endicott, Samuel, 74
Ends, Elizabeth (Mrs. John Brothers), 46
Episcopal Church (Alexandria) 4, 29, 34, 84, 93, 96

Faw, Mary Ann, 24-25
Fairfax, Rev. Bryan (Lord), 61
Fairfax County (Virginia), 2, 23, 31, 40, 61, 65, 66, 68
Fendall, Philip R., 33
Fendall, II, Philip R., 41
Finley, Rev. Robert, 50
First Presbyterian Church (Alexandria, District of Columbia and Virginia), 103. *See also* Old Presbyterian Meeting House
First Presbyterian Church (Baltimore), 24, 37-40, 59, 73, 92
First Presbyterian Church (New York City), 45
First Presbyterian Church (St. Andrew's, National Presbyterian, Washington, D.C.), 92
Fitzhugh, Lucy Carter (Mrs. William), 65-66
Fitzhugh, Nicholas, 79

Fitzhugh, William, 65-66
Fleming, Andrew, 74
Fleming, Catherine Steele (Mrs. Andrew), 74
Flounder House, 2, 43. *See* parsonage
Foote, Rev. John, 55
Forbes, William (Jamaica), 71, 73, 74, 76, 81
Friendship Fire Co., 71
Funeral services, 5, 7, 24, 33, 34, 37, 38, 40, 45, 60, 66, 68, 69, 70, 73, 95, 96, 97, 99, 101

Gadsby, John, 24-25
Gadsby, Margaret Smelt (Mrs. John), 24-25
Gadsby's Tavern, 9, 25, 30, 45, 46, 48-49, 53
General Assembly (Presbyterian Church in the U.S.A.), 12, 15, 37, 38, 44, 45-50, 52, 55, 56, 59, 91, 97
General Association. *See* Congregational Churches in Connecticut
Georgetown (District of Columbia), 7, 37, 43, 51, 63, 72-73, 74, 92, 100
Georgetown (Bridge-Street) Presbyterian Church (District of Columbia), 34, 73-74, 92, 101
Glasgow, University of (Scotland), 10, 87
Glendy, Rev. John, 34, 38, 39, 45, 70
Goodrich, Rev. Samuel, 55-56
Goodrich, Russell, 57
Gray, Robert and John, 17, 89, 98
Green, Rev. Ashbel, 45-46, 48, 52, 57, 64, 68-69, 75, 81
Guilford (Connecticut), 49, 55, 57

Hamilton, Alexander, 8, 21-22, 37
Harper, John, 51
Harper, Robert Goodloe, 27
Harper, William, 32
Harrison, Rev. Elias, 41, 103
Hartshorne, William, 33, 61, 71
Hall, Nancy Grace Craig (Mrs. William), 83
Hall, William James, 83
Hill, Jane Perry (Mrs. Laurence),

78
Hill, Laurence, 78
Hill, Mary (Mrs. John Parker), 76
Hill, Rev. William, 51, 81, 83
Hunt, Rev. James, 96
Hunter, Cordelia Meeks Hatton (Mrs. John), 21
Hunter, Rev. Henry, 10, 79
Hunter, John, 21
Inglis, Rev. James, 32-33, 38-39, 45, 48, 70-72, 73, 74, 77, 80, 91-92
Irvin, James, 50, 61, 68, 83
Jamieson, Andrew, 8, 23-24, 44-46, 47, 48, 62, 71, 76, 77, 78, 83, 86
Jamieson, Mary Sweet (Mrs. Andrew), 24
Jews, 69, 79
Johnston, Christopher, 38-41, 74, 77
Johnston, Jane S. (Mrs. James Inglis), 92
Jura, Mary (Mrs. John Dixon), 41
Keith, Rev. Isaac Stockton, 62, 76, 102
Kennedy, James, 71-72
Key, Francis Scott, 30, 40
Knox, Rev. Samuel, 73
Ladd, Elizabeth (Mrs. John Gardner), 72
Ladd, John Gardner, 72
Legrand, Rev. Nash, 54-55
Lee, Charles, 25, 29, 68
Lee, Edmund Jennings, 25, 32, 59, 67, 68-69, 78
Lee, Francis Lightfoot, 88
Lee, Richard Bland, 25, 51, 68, 83
Lee, Sarah (Mrs. Edmund Jennings), 69
Leesburg (Virginia), 22, 28, 35
Lenox, Robert, 45-46, 52, 57-58
Liberty Hall (Washington and Lee University), 81
London (England), 10, 21, 42, 67, 73, 79, 84, 89-90
Lord's Day, *See* Sabbath Day School, worship services
Lord's Supper, service of the (Communion), 6, 28, 32, 34, 35, 36, 39, 72, 74, 76
Lowry, William, 62
Lyles, Enoch M., 37, 64-66
Lyles, Henry, 77
Lyon, Andrew, 31
Maffitt, Henrietta Turberville (Mrs. William), 7, 8, 23, 34, 40, 42, 45
Maffitt, Rev. William, 2, 7, 23, 24, 25, 29, 34, 42, 45, 50, 51, 60, 67, 68, 71, 75, 76, 79, 81-83
Marriage services, 5, 7, 22, 23, 31, 31, 46, 51, 63, 67, 74, 75, 76, 77, 101
Martin, Luther, 27
Martin, William, 75
Masonic Lodge No. 22, Alexandria-Washington, 13, 60, 85-87
services at Meeting House, 85-87
Massachusetts Society for Promoting Christian Knowledge (MSPCK), 62
Massey, Mary (Mrs. Andrew Lyon), 31
Mattson, Rev. Enoch, 88
Meeting House, *See* Old Presbyterian Meeting House
McGehanny, __, 42, 44
McHenry, James, 39-40
McKinney, John, 32
Methodist Church, 5, 36, 88
Middletown (Connecticut), 50, 57, 67
Miller, Rev. Samuel, 59, 77
Mills, John, 42, 73, 79, 89-90
Missionary Magazine, General Assembly's, 5, 46, 52, 64, 69, 70, 75, 81-83, 98, 99
Missions, 12, 46, 47, 48 *See also Missionary Magazine*
Monthly Visitant, 16, 100, 102
Morgan, Mary (Mrs. William C. R. Smith), 63
Morse, Rev. Jedidiah, 15, 52, 62-63, 67, 72
Muir, Elizabeth Love, 2, 12
Muir, Elizabeth Welman (Mrs. James), 1, 8, 10, 12, 24, 44, 91
Muir, Rev. James, *passim*.
biographical sketch, 10-16

image of diary page, 19
personal diary, 21-93
portrait of, 11
publications by, 95-101
sermon Bible texts, 94
silhouette of, i
Muir, Jane Wardlaw, 2, 12, 47, 88, 90-91
Muir, John, 78
Muir, Mary (Mrs. John), 78
Muir, Mary Wardlaw, 2, 8, 12, 26 32, 44, 46, 47, 50, 90-91
Muir, Samuel Crichton, 2, 8-10, 12, 23, 24, 29, 45, 46, 68, 81, 83
National (St. Andrew's, First) Presbyterian Church (Washington, D.C.), 92
Newbold, Captain William W., 26, 44, 90
New Haven (Connecticut), 55, 56-57, 59
New York City (New York), 3, 7, 12, 22, 43, 45, 50-53, 57-59, 71, 91
Nicholas, Lewis, 30, 62

Old Presbyterian Meeting House (Alexandria, District of Columbia and Virginia), 102-105, *passim.*, *see also* baptismal services, Burial Ground, funeral services, parsonage, wedding services, and worship services
    Church Committee, 21, 34, 36, 39, 45, 50, 62, 72, 77, 78, 87, 91, 112
    image of Meeting House, 105
Oliver, Robert, 40-43

Panoplist, 5, 62- 64, 65, 67, 70, 71, 72, 76, 78, 79, 81, 84, 98, 99
Parker, John, 76
Parsonage, 1, 2, 4, 10, 33, 42-43, 49, 75
Patton, James 81
Patton, William, 70-71
Patton, Mary Roberdeau (Mrs. William), 70-71
Pearce, Gideon, 76
Pendleton, Nathaniel, 22
Peter, John, 63, 84

Philadelphia (Pennsylvania), 3, 4, 7, 12, 27, 45, 46-48, 49, 51, 52, 55, 59, 64, 67, 74, 75, 83, 95, 96, 100
Philologos (Rev. James Muir), 5, 72, 98, 99
Plan of Union (between Congregational and Presbyterian denominations), 48, 49
Potomac River, 3, 4, 8, 9, 22, 29, 63, 65
"shut up" (frozen solid), 8, 21-22, 24
Presbyterian Cemetery (Alexandria) *See* Burial Ground
Presbyterian Church in the U.S.A., *passim.*, *see also* General Assembly, Presbyteries by name, College of New Jersey, *Missionary Magazine*, Princeton Theological Seminary, Synods of Kentucky, Philadelphia and Virginia, and individual congregations by name
Presbyterian Church (Alexandria), *See* Old Presbyterian Meeting House
Presbytery of Baltimore (Presbyterian Church in the U.S.A.), 5, 12, 15, 23, 27, 34, 35, 36-38, 45-46, 50, 70, 73, 74, 88, 92, 98, 100
Presbytery of Cumberland, 56
Presbytery of Transylvania, 97
Presbytery of Winchester (Presbyterian Church in the U.S.A.), 35, 54, 92
Price, Molly, 23, 43
Princeton (New Jersey), 7, 37, 59
Princeton Day School, 37
Princeton Theological Seminary, 45, 58, 59
Princeton University, *See* College of New Jersey

Quakers (Society of Friends), 5, 31, 33

Ramsay, William, 61
Relief Society (Relief Fire Co.), Alexandria, 12
Revivals, religious, 6, 35-36, 56-57
Richards, Jane (Mrs. John) 87
Richards, John, 87

Riddle, James, 87
Riddle, Joseph, 72, 76, 80, 87
Riddle, Sarah Morrow Kersley (Mrs. Joseph), 72
Robbery, 63, 84
Robbins, Rev. Thomas, 47-48
Rodgers, Rev. John, 12, 50, 52-53, 57, 59
Rose, Henry, 32

Sabbath Day School, 12, 103
Salmon, George, 39
Scotland, 3, 10, 21, 24, 44, 45, 52, 72, 92
Scott, James S., 25
Scott, May Adgate (Mrs. James), 25
Second Presbyterian Church (Alexandria), 51, 103, 104
Second Presbyterian Church (Baltimore), 34, 37, 39
Second Presbyterian Church (Philadelphia), 46, 52, 55
Servants, 1, 23, 27, 42, 43, 50, 55, 88
Services, *See* worship services
Shuck, Frederick, 33
Simms, Charles, 13
Simms, William Douglass, 29-30
Slavery (and anti-slavery), 3, 4, 15, 31, 103, *see also* African American
Smith, Alexander, 32
Smith, Rev. Robert, 102
Smith, Rev. Samuel Stanhope, 59
Smith, William C. R., 63
Spence, Rev. Conrad, 34, 38, 39, 42, 73-74
Stewart, Elizabeth Dunlop (Mrs. James A.), 26
Stewart, James A., x, 17, 26
Stewart, Jane, (Mrs. John A.), 26
Stewart, John A., 26
Stewart, Mary, 26, 40, 40, 43, 44, 70, 90, 91
St. Andrew's Society of Alexandria, 13, 24, 80-81
  service at Old Presbyterian Meeting House, 80-81
St. Andrew's Society of New York City, 45, 53

St. John's (Episcopal) Church (Broad Creek, Maryland), 65
Sully Estate (Fairfax County, Virginia), 51, 68, 83
Swift, Ann Foster Roberdeau (Mrs. Jonathan), 37
Swift, Jonathan, 32, 36-37, 48, 63, 64, 78
Synod of Kentucky (Presbyterian Church in the U.S.A.), 56-57
Synod of Philadelphia (Presbyterian Church in the U.S.A.), 12, 46, 97
Synod of Virginia (Presbyterian Church in the U.S.A.), 35

Thom, Rev. William, 102
Thompson, Jonah, 32-33
Thompson, Martha Peyton (Mrs. Jonah), 33
Tillary, James, 52, 58, 59
Tucker, Captain John, 26, 44, 69

Union Presbyterian Church (Alexandria) 103

Van Hess, William, 22
Veitch, Elizabeth (Mrs. George Bowling), 31
Vowell, Mary Harper (Mrs. Thomas), 49, 65, 68-70
Vowell, Thomas, 49, 65, 68-70, 76-77, 81, 82, 84

Washburn, Rev. Joseph, 79-82, 86
Washington, George, 12, 13, 14, 16, 25, 29-30, 31, 39, 62, 102, 104
Washington Society of Alexandria, 12, 23, 27, 29-30, 37, 40, 59, 62, 66, 68, 88, 99, 100
Watson, Josiah, 66
Watson, Mary, 66
Weather conditions, 8, 17-18, 21, 22, 25, 26, 28, 29, 31, 35, 60, 79, 89, 92-93
Welman, Captain Samuel, 26, 44, 61, 90-91
Welman, Elizabeth, *See* Muir, Elizabeth Welman (Mrs. James)
Welman, Margaret Harvey (Mrs. Samuel), 44
Welman, Robert, 33, 45, 90-91

Wheeler, Samuel, 67
Wiley, Rev. David, 45, 47, 76, 82, 91-92
Williams, Captain Benjamin, 56, 67
Williams, Martha Cornell (Mrs. Benjamin), 55-56
Williams, William Joseph, x, 11
Williamson, Rev. William, 28, 35, 36, 51, 91, 92
Wilson, Elizabeth Johnston Taylor (Mrs. James), 44
Wilson, James, 44, 60, 78
Winbefield, Winifred (Mrs. Samuel Wheeler), 68
Winchester Presbyterian Church (Winchester, Virginia), 51, 81
Witherspoon, Rev. John, 10, 95, 102
Woodrow, Mary (Mrs. William Martin), 76
Worship services, 4-8, 13-14, 103-105, *passim., see also* Lord's Supper
   at midweek, 5, 6, 24, 25, 31, 36, 42, 51, 73, 80, 81, 85
   Bible texts for sermons by Rev. Muir listed, 93
   for charity, 5 13, 85, 87, 102
   on Christmas Day, 87
   on Easter, 41
   on St. Andrew's Day, 80-81

Yale College, 8, 16, 53, 54-55, 58
Yeaton, William, 47
Young, Elizabeth Mary, 41
Young, Elizabeth Mary Conrad, (Mrs. Robert), 41
Young, Gen. Robert, 35, 41
Young, Rev. Robert, 79-80

About the Editor

Donald C. Dahmann is a geographer in independent practice. He holds a doctorate from the University of Chicago, and formerly served as a geographer with the U.S. Census Bureau and the National Academy of Sciences in Washington, D.C., and as topographic engineer and director of the Liberia-United States Mapping Mission in Liberia, West Africa. His previous publications are in human geography, the history of geography, and on urban settlement. He is an elder in the Presbyterian Church U.S.A., a member of the Old Presbyterian Meeting House congregation, and the former chair of the Meeting House's History and Archives committee.

www.ingramcontent.com/pod-product-compliance
Lightning Source LLC
Chambersburg PA
CBHW070457090426
42735CB00012B/2592